FORGETTING THE MONEY:

10 Step Framework to Harness True Project Value

Forgetting the Money

Money

10 Step Framework to Harness True Project Value

BY DINA GOFMAN

PROJECT
ACCOUNTING
AUSTRALIA

Forgetting the Money: 10 Step Framework to Harness True Project Value ©
2018 | Project Accounting Australia Pty Ltd

ISBN: 978-0-646-99668-4

Acknowledgements

There are so many people that I want to thank that this section could almost be as long as the book itself.

To everyone in my long list of References whose works have inspired me and given this book its purpose. To my mentor, business partner and most wonderful friend Lourdes Duggineni, whose ideas are in this text as much as mine, – thank you for all your support. To my incredible mentors whose feedback and attention to detail with each draft I sent over really brought out the practical application of this book. A special mention goes to John Dowey, whose patience and countless hours on this book have truly challenged me. To all the project accountants out there who have shared themselves with me over the years – thank you for all that you do!

On a personal note, I want to thank my parents for their support and inspiration, plus for looking after my one-year old so that I could put my passion to paper. To my sister turned marketing manager, editor and publisher who turned my ideas into a readable book. And there could not be greater gratitude to my partner, Gennadi Gofman, for his endless love and encouragement to see this book through. Thank you!

To Hannah,

Whilst you were sleeping...

Contents

Prologue

For the past decade, I have been hired by organisations across multiple sectors – Financial Services, Regulatory, Insurance, Property and Engineering – to fix their project finances. I'd go into organisations in order to fix the same broken processes (or lack there-of) in order to financially manage projects. With all the project delivery approaches and methodologies out there, you would think that the project or accounting fields would have worked out a standardised approach to dealing with complex delivery, to ensure transparency and to manage financial risk. That is not the case.

The main reason for this is that managing project finance is seen as an innovation blocker or hindrance, and is pushed back by teams and processes. This perception stems from the notion that accountants hinder project progress because organisations care too much about budgets. My personal pet peeve was when consultants brought in the latest "newest and greatest" delivery approach with zero guidance on how to look after these projects financially and track both the cost and value derived on an ongoing basis.

And every year, we hear the media cover this story – a story of a large project that a company decided to invest in that failed. Several project specialists were brought in; development teams were working on various aspects of creation, and the idea was to simplify or innovate something. After a few years in the making, with over millions of dollars in spend, the company had to announce to the market that they failed. A bunch of people were let go, the auditors wrote several reports for improvements in required controls, consultants were brought in to fix it and if lucky the company continued to trade with 'business as usual'.

This story however is not just an occasional panic; more often the company covers and hides this, no matter the cost. In reality, this kind of failure is as high as 70% for in-house projects (based on Project Accounting Australia's experience) and as high as 97% in the start-up and complex problem-solving sphere. After seeing this time and time again and knowing that this financial wastage can be prevented, or at least reduced, I decided it's time to take action towards incorporated project finances from the outset.

Forgetting the Money: 10 step framework to harness true project value brings together the various learnings that minimises financial risks of failure, increases transparency and drives project success. Any organisation or team can implement all 10 steps, but even picking or choosing some of the steps will help achieve outcomes for your desired output.

A big thank you to the entire project accounting community for their input and their continuous innovation in this field. Particular and significant thank you to Project Accounting Australia's co-founder Lourdes Duggineni for her invaluable expertise and input into this framework.

Dina Gofman

What is Project Accounting?

Project Accounting (sometimes called Project Management Accounting) is a specialised form of accounting that corresponds to the ever-evolving needs of project delivery, which helps track, report and analyse financial results and implications. Project accounting arose due to the high financial repercussions of project failure.

Research by McKinsey and University of Oxford on 5,400 large IT projects (Brown, et al., 2016), found:

- half of all participating projects had large budget overruns (overall total cost blowouts near AUD 66 billion);
- on average, these projects ran 45% over initial budgets and delivered 56% less value than original scope; and
- the longer the time allocated to a project, the more likely it was that it would run over the allocated time and initial budget (Bloch, et al., 2012).

A project is defined as a separate temporary individualised entity set up for the purpose of delivering one or more business products (AXELOS Limited, 2014). As separate entities, projects come with the complexities of running separate individual companies, which sit within an existing business structure. The need for project accounting arose to ensure that these separate new entities deliver in the interests of the existing sponsoring business and abide by their respective industry benchmarks, laws and regulations. The nature of each project is different to the business-as-usual activities run by the business, which creates additional business and financial risk. Existing management and financial accounting skills are recognised as insufficient to advise on the treatment and financial reporting of a project. Hence, a new field emerged within the accounting sphere – project accounting.

Traditionally, project accounting and its principles were used to track and report large construction, engineering and government projects. Today, project management delivery approaches have expanded into several other sectors, including financial, technology and legal.

Subsequently, project accounting evolved to cover these industries ensuring corresponding financial tracking and financial implications are understood and considered.

The project accounting field requires knowledge of management accounting, financial accounting, cross-functional involvement, and understand project delivery approaches used by the business. The Project Accountant plays a *Translator* role between the Project team and other Accounting

The Project Accountant TAG
Translator
Advisor
Gatekeeper

functions. Acting as *Advisor* i.e. advising the project team on the financial treatment and implications of the decisions being made, their impact on both the project and the business, and, *Gatekeeper* i.e. reporting into the business the true and fair view of how the project is tracking.

Over the past decade, those businesses that have looked at including project accounting as part of their project delivery frameworks have seen an increase in project transparency, ease of decision-making and a substantial increase in project success.

This book is also a Project Accounting Framework (framework), which provides guidance in standardising processes, structures and functions required in a business to improve project transparency, governance and decision making. This framework will guide you through these steps:

1. Governance
2. Planning
3. Impact: CAPEX and Value
4. Workforce management
5. Tracking
6. Systems
7. Benefits and OPEX
8. Reporting
9. Portfolio and prioritisation
10. Review and improvement

To gain the most out of this framework, the business will require the integration of a Project Accountant or a Project Accounting team (dependent on the size of your business) within its Finance or Accounting department.

However, acknowledging where the organisational appetite for investment into such a function may be limited, this book will guide existing Accountants and Project Managers on how to take advantage of project accounting best practices.

KEY TAKEAWAYS

- Project Accounting arose due to the financial repercussions of project failure. This is why implementing the Project Accounting Framework can increase project success.

- Project Accountants act as Translators, Advisors and Gatekeepers.

- This Project Accounting (PA) Framework is divided into 10 steps which offer guidance in standardising processes, structures and functions required in a business to improve project transparency, governance and decision making. This is required for project success from a financial point of view.

Step 1: Governance

Partnership and independence must be considered to ensure successful financial governance, to avoid conflicts and skewed information. Your business should have a project delivery team that works closely with the Accounting department. The Project Accountant working with the project should remain independent from the project itself, i.e. by reporting into the Accounting department. This is due to a potential conflict of interest and the need for transparency in reporting.

In practice: regardless of the Project Accountant's independence from the Project team or Accounting department, it is imperative for this role to manage both the Project and Accounting stakeholders in a manner where their role is clearly understood by both.

1.1 Project delivery approaches

Prior to establishing financial project governance, a project delivery approach must be given consideration. Regardless of which project delivery approach is chosen by the project or the business, all mention financial reporting as part of project tracking and business case/lean canvas development processes to some extent.

This framework proposes that the way financials are tracked and reported to the business are more meaningful and consistent if driven by Project Accountant(s). This is due to the role that the Project Accountant plays in *translating* a project's financial implications into accounting standards driven reporting. If a Project Accountant is not available, appropriate training is required for either the Accountant or Project personnel responsible for the project finance and accounting of a project.

- *Waterfall approach* – each milestone or stage gate is assessed whether value is being created by the project. This will help determine whether the project is creating an asset or is an expense made by the business.

The basic project lifecycle within such a delivery approach would look as follows:

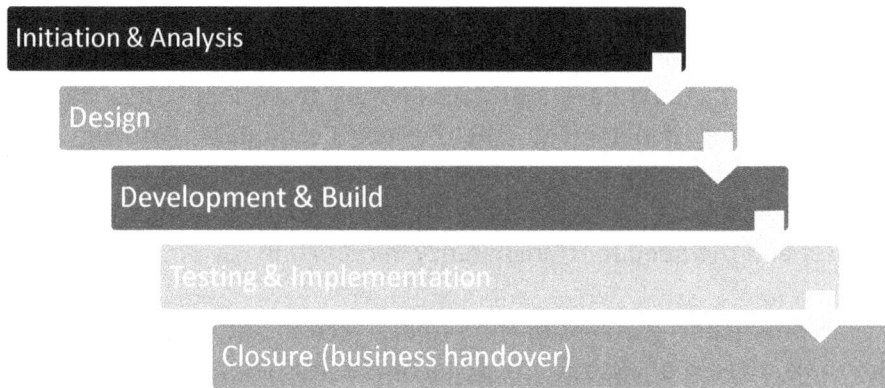

- *Agile delivery approach* – each iteration is assessed whether value has been delivered as per accounting standards and internal policies. This will determine whether the iteration has created, or is creating, an asset for the business; or whether the iteration is an operational / business-as-usual activity. The basic project lifecycle within such a delivery framework would look as follows:

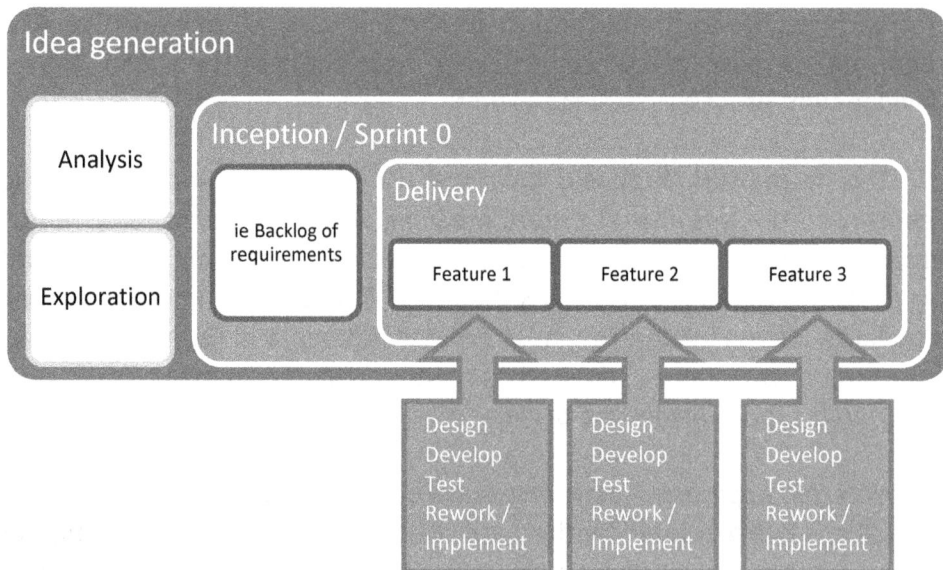

- *Hybrid delivery approach* – agile delivery approach may deliver a milestone or stage gate within a waterfall delivery approach. Here, the Project Accountant will work closely with the delivery team to determine an assessable mechanism to assess the nature of the deliverable. There are many variations to this project lifecycle. For simplicity, when the Hybrid delivery approach is referred to in this book, the reader should note it is a collaboration of both the waterfall delivery approach and agile delivery approach in some working form.

1.2 Role definition

Project delivery approaches may recommend the roles required from a financial assurance perspective. This framework complements these approaches, where they recommend functions required for financial assurance. This framework goes further in recommending practical key roles involved in delivering and tracking the value derived by the project, which would complement the project delivery approach in use.

We propose that the business defines these roles to include:

1. *Project Accountant* – helps track and report the value created by the Project. This book refers to the role of the Project Accountant through a **TAG** acronym:

   Translator role between the Project and other Accounting functions;

   Advisor role advising the Project team on the financial treatment and implications of the decisions being made, their impact on both the project and the business; and

   Gatekeeper role reporting into the business the true and fair view of how the project is tracking financially.

2. *Project Management Office(r) (PMO) (recommended)* – provides governance and risk management through the facilitation of project prioritisation and approvals process. This role provides *guidance* in defining tools, templates and processes to develop and maintain a standardised approach. Project Accountants partner with the PMO to provide holistic insights about Projects to facilitate decision making.

The following two roles are deemed as optional, as these depend on the size of the business, project, available tools and delivery approach chosen.

3. *Portfolio Personnel (optional)* – this role merges all project financial information to provide a portfolio view of the business. This role can be performed by the Project Accountant and has a recommended dual reporting line into the Accounting function and PMO.

Pros: Maintains a holistic portfolio view of all projects at play and helps ease prioritisation.

Cons: This is an extra cost to the organisation and provided the portfolio is small enough, can be maintained by existing Project Accountants and PMO.

4. *Master Scheduler (optional)* – this role has an overall view of all portfolio deliverables across the organisation and maintains a master interdependency register. This role validates and provides assurance of timelines, dependencies and risks across the entire portfolio. In doing so, this role assists in decision making for resource and funding allocation. This role would report to either the PMO, Assurance or Risk in any business.

Pros: Helps ensure that multiple projects are in sync with each other and are able to be delivered with the resources on hand.

Cons: This function can be largely self-managed by the PMO and Project Managers provided software is used appropriately and consistently across the organisation.

1.3 Accountability

There are different segments of accountability for a project depending on the delivery approach chosen by the organisation or project, or the size of the organisation. The segments of accountability are split into:

1. *Executive Board[1]* – this is the key leadership, who allocate the funding for investment into projects. This team maintains accountability to the shareholders of the organisation and handles disclosure of investments made.

This team will appoint a Project Board or a Project Sponsor to take responsibility for individual projects or programs.

---

[1] This segment is referred to by many names throughout the corporate world i.e. corporate or programme management (AXELOS Limited, 2014); the leadership team of the organisation; or Business Owners.

The subsequent segments diverge dependent on project delivery approach:

Waterfall Accountability (AXELOS Limited, 2014)	Agile Accountability (Agile42, 2016)
2. *Project Board* – handles the overall direction and management of the project within the constraints set out by the *Executive Board*. This team is accountable for the success of the project. 3. *Project Manager* – handles the day-to-day management of the project within the constraints set out by the *Project Board*. 4. *Delivery Team* – handles the delivery of the project's product within the scope, time, quality and cost.	2. *Project Sponsor (recommended)* – is the business entity, whether a division or an individual interested in the successful delivery of the project for the business. This role mainly exists in larger organisations creating a buffer between the Executive Board and the Product Owner. 3. There are 3 co-equal Scrum Team roles which together maintain the accountability for the project: a) *Product Owner* – handles the interface between the *Delivery Team* and the stakeholders of the project i.e. *Project Sponsor*. The key responsibility of this role is for the return on investment (ROI) of the project. b) *Scrum Master* – ensures that the *Delivery Team* adheres to the Scrum theory, practices and rules. c) *Delivery Team* –is responsible to deliver the committed delivery in time and with the defined quality. It is a stand-alone body self-managing the delivery.

1.4 Delegation, approvals & thresholds

Waterfall approach

The Waterfall approach acts based on constraints and boundaries. If, or when, the project requires further funding, it will need to gain approval from the level above (standard practice is 5-10% leniency). This creates a hierarchical environment for delegations of authority given to each segment for the decision-making process. See ***Example 1.1***.

Example 1.1: The Project Manager realises that by committing to a contract with a new vendor, the project is going to overspend by 10% of its budget. The Project Manager will have to seek the Project Board's permission to do so.

In this case, the Project Accountant (through liaising with the Accounting division) will help make recommendations to the Project Board as to whether the overall business budget of the organisation can accommodate the additional funds to close the required 10% gap for the project.

This framework recommends that the organisation maintain a clear delegation of authority for financial threshold approvals if this is the dominant delivery approach chosen by the organisation. Please see below an example of a $100,000 project:

Delegation of Authority	Can Approve/Commit to
Executive Board	>$110,000
Project Board	Up to $110,000 i.e. 10% more
Project Manager	Up to $100,000
Delivery Team	Nothing

Agile delivery approach

The agile delivery approach takes a risk-based approach to deliver the project. This means that before committing to a contract or a large amount of spending, there will be a pilot or first Sprint to test the viability of the solution. Given a finite amount of funds, the project will deliver a minimal viable product. From this, determining how much a minimal viable product will cost becomes critical in determining the approvals process. This book presents one such approach to how delegations of authority for agile projects can work. *See **Example 1.2.***

Example 1.2: The Executive Board decides that in the next financial year there will be a $1m allocation to projects in the organisation. After going through the Scrum estimation process and Sprint Zero, the Product Owner estimates that the minimal viable product will cost $100,000. This is the amount drawn down from allocated $1m to projects.

Once the Product Owner sees that the project is progressing well and there are further benefits to be gained from funding further iterations, the Product Owner will request further funding draw-downs within the $1m allocation.

In this case, the Project Accountant's role is to ensure that draw downs of the $1m are being utilised toward the highest ROI. Hence, recommending whether funding should continue for this specific project.

Based on **Example 1.2**, this framework recommends that the organisation's approach to delegations of authority for financial threshold approvals remains flexible. The approvals for further funding should be determined by the opportunity cost of investing in the existing project versus another project dependant on the ROI of each investment. Please see below for an example of a $100,000 project:

Delegation of Authority	Can Approve/Commit to
Executive Board	<$1m in Overall Portfolio Project Spend for the Financial Year
Product Owner	Up to $100,000

1.5 Internal controls

Internal controls may be implied or documented, dependent on the size of the business and project delivery approach used by the project. Internal controls ensure that the Project is transparent and delivers within defined/approved controls that the business has endorsed. Internal controls allow the business to validate the Project processes are functioning and hence, decrease business and operational risk. This book will not go into details of required internal controls as these will often be guided by internal policies of the organisation. The audit function will often help determine whether internal controls are adequate to minimise the risks associated with Project delivery.

KEY TAKEAWAYS

- A Project Accountant must maintain independence.

- Value generation is the most important aspect of *translating* project delivery approach into financial implications for the project and organisation.

- It is important to determine the appropriate financial delegation and accountability.

Step 2: Planning

As part of planning for project delivery, one of the main points of consideration is project funding. Independent of which project delivery approach is chosen, funding must be obtained to pursue the idea the project is looking to deliver.

Whether a project is being funded externally by a client, investor or bank; or internally by your organisation, the person/team generating the idea will compile the initial documentation showing consideration as to why it is worth pursuing the idea. Many aspects are worth considering as part of this initial documentation. This book will briefly describe the minimum aspects of such documentation, which will allow for ease of decision-making. Below we look at some points of consideration when making this choice.

2.1 Business Case vs Lean Canvas

Having initial documentation helps the project team articulate their idea in a way that is understandable to their stakeholders.

There are several descriptions of both business case and lean canvas. The variations of these descriptions must be considered when implementing these in your organisation and/or for your project. This book will give a limited introduction into these descriptions and examples of how these are being used in industry.

- *Business Case* refers to an argument or justification usually used to convince a decision maker to approve an action. Waterfall defines a business case as a document which "typically contains costs, benefits, risks and timescales, against which continuing viability is tested" (AXELOS Limited, 2014).
- *Lean Canvas* refers to an adaptation of the Business Model Canvas[2] by Alexander Osterwalder, which Ash Maurya created in the Lean Start-up (Ries, 2011) spirit. Although targeted at entrepreneurs as an "actionable

---

[2] Please refer to https://strategyzer.com/canvas/business-model-canvas for further information.

and entrepreneur-focused business plan" (Maurya, 2012), for larger projects and/or organisations it has been an overview document compiled instead of or complementing the Business Case. We have predominantly seen these used as part of the *Agile delivery approach.*

The uses of either a Business Case or a Lean Canvas both have their advantages and disadvantages. Both tools require continuous updating to ensure their usefulness in describing the most up-to-date scope, quality, time and funding required for delivery.

When considering whether a Business Case or a Lean Canvas is more appropriate for a potential project, consideration should be given to project delivery approach, the potential size, complexity and value of the project. The bigger or more complex the potential project, the more likely it is that a Business Case will be requested or used. This is not because a Business Case is superior to a Lean Canvas, especially in the initial stages of a project; from observation, it is mainly because a Business Case has:

- A lot more detail in it, forcing the project manager to think through every aspect of the idea proposed and document it, regardless of how wrong or out-dated this document may become even a month into the project;
- The visual representation of a large document when asking for a large amount of funding comforts the approver (Kahneman, 2011), regardless of whether the document contains relevant information; and
- Historical use of the *Waterfall approach* and familiarity with it places confidence on large Business Cases, regardless of how statistically unsuccessful these have been in delivering the promised scope within time, budget and quality, specifically for IT projects (Sweeney, 2014).

The Lean Canvas comes with its own challenges as well, whereby it often has insufficient information to ensure appropriate decision making for both financial and longer-term projects.

This framework proposes that if a Lean Canvas is chosen as the initial document that the value of the project is not given a "ballpark" metric or number, but that thorough thought goes into these initial estimates.

Please refer to *2.2 Original Estimation or Initial Budget* for ways this can be done.

Similar to there being several project delivery approaches i.e. agile, waterfall and hybrid, in project management, there are several distinct accounting environments. These ways of working depend on whether the organisation's Accounting function has worked within the *standard* accounting environment; within a *lean* accounting environment[3]; or somewhere between the two ways of working, namely also a *hybrid* of sorts. Dependant on the accounting environment chosen by the organisation, a different amount of information will be required for financial budgeting and planning purposes at different times during the project lifecycle. Please see *Example 1.3* for the way this works in practice.

---

[3] Please refer to http://davidparmenter.com for further information.

Example 1.3:

Standard accounting environment will require a *locked in* project budget view several months prior to financial year end. Business Cases, unlike lean canvases, are generally built to accommodate this environment. Your project will always be compared to this budget, no matter how out of date it will become. **NB.** Some organisations use Change Controls/Requests to change or track budget amendments.

Lean accounting environment will require an *estimate guideline* of the project budget for the next year/quarter approximately a month prior to financial year end. Every financial year quarter, the project budget for the upcoming quarter is defined based on the workload to be achieved in that quarter and this ends up being your Key Performance Indicator (KPI). Lean canvases are generally enough to accommodate this environment if they are continuously updated on a quarterly basis.

Hybrid accounting environment can work in a variety of ways. There are several variations on this environment. One of the more common environments will expect an *initial* project budget view a few months prior to financial year end. On a quarterly basis this budget will be *modified* and new KPIs will be set, against which the project will be tracked. Both the Business Case and Lean Canvas suit this environment, provided these are continuously updated, whether on a quarterly or materiality basis.

2.2 Original Estimation or Initial Budget

Regardless of many project management books and blogs stating that an estimate should be just that - an estimate the consensus among accountants and other project stakeholders is this estimate will often lock in the project into a budget. When Project Managers or Scrum Teams embark on their initial estimation process to allow for budget setting for a project, one of two ways is used:

1. **Absolute Estimation** (aka Guesstimate) based on the general scope, time and resources required by the project, individual stage gate or stream of the project. This is called an "educated guess" using units of time and if available, vendor quotes if purchases are required for a project component. Arguably, unless the project is being replicated from a previously existing project, these estimates are nowhere close to what the project ultimately costs. Hence, the project team will also ask for a percentage contingency on top of this estimate (percentage of contingency may differ even further depending on levels of confidence, etc).

Where this approach becomes more challenging is if the project spans multiple financial years. For appropriate budgeting to happen for such a project, the Project Accountant ensures that during the time of budget setting, the latest information is allowed for.

Please note where your organisation uses lean accounting - annual budgets will be indicative estimates only and rarely form part of your KPIs until the upcoming financial quarter in which the work is forecast to be done (Parmenter, 2016). This allows for a more mobile approach to project accounting.

2. **Agile Estimation** (aka Relative Estimation) is based on the *agile* way of working. This way of estimating is based on relative work effort and has several techniques available[4]. One of the most common methods of agile estimation is Planning Poker, which uses a

---

[4] Please refer to http://www.agileadvice.com/2015/10/13/agilemanagement/9-agile-estimation-techniques/ for further information.

Fibonacci-like format i.e. 0, 0.5, 1, 2, 3, 5, 8, 13, 20, 40, 100 & infinity/unknown to allocate Story Points to the required tasks at hand. It is widely used by many Scrum professionals and is based on the previous experiences of the entire cross-functional team involved in the delivery the project. This ensures that the estimation process is not left to one person i.e. Project Manager and maintains the team's involvement and responsibility for the estimation.

The main differentiating factor for using Story Points is that complexity of each task is considered and the velocity (speed of the team to complete the points) is the measurement used by the team. Unfortunately, velocity rarely corresponds to hours, days or weeks. The relationship between points and hours is a distribution. One Story Point equals a distribution with a mean of x and some standard deviation (Cohn, 2014). This is not an intuitive process for most people, which is why this book strongly recommends training in Agile Estimation if this is the main method used by your organisation or project. Noting the above, the first pilot Sprint sets up an initial estimate, which together with consecutive Sprints are used for estimation of project velocity and cost of Sprints to come. Please refer to **Example 1.4** for a simplified example of the way agile estimation is used.

Example 1.4:

You have a banana, an apple and a pineapple to make a fruit salad. Assuming you don't know how long it will take you, or how granular the client wants the fruit salad sliced. The following steps will guide you through the process:

1. Assume the Scrum team agrees with the baseline that preparing a banana for a fruit salad is 2 Points worth of work. You can be assume that this is a relatively easy process i.e. peel the banana, slice the banana and put into the salad bowl.

2. Based on the banana preparation equalling 2 Points of work, preparing an apple can be deemed a little harder i.e. cut the apple, core the apple, slice the apple and put into the salad bowl. The Scrum team would probably agree that the apple is likely to be 3 Points of work.

3. Based on the banana and apple allocation of Points, the pineapple preparation will likely be deemed much harder to estimate. There will likely be dependencies, such as the equipment available or whether the pineapple is required to be fresh or canned. These will likely be debated in the Scrum team as to the various experiences that the team had with preparing a pineapple. In the end, the Scrum team may seek further information or allocate an amount of Points based on an assumption i.e. 13 Points assuming a fresh pineapple.

2 Points   3 Points   13 Points

4. Now that we have agreed on the Story Points, let us Pilot the first Sprint during which the Scrum team has decided that it can only tackle the banana. The banana took 4 minutes to prepare where we know that 4 minutes of the Scrum team's time is $4 based on $1 per minute.

Sprint 1 = 2 Points = 4 minutes = $4

Example 1.4 (continued):

5. As each activity is relative when estimating the monetary or time equivalent of each Story Point, we must consider a range of time and monetary value it may take to deliver each Sprint (Cohn, 2014). Based on the above steps, the Scrum team can make the following estimation:

> Apple: 3 Points = 5-7 minutes = $5-7
> Pineapple: 13 Points = 20-30 minutes = $20-$30
> **Total Project Estimate**
> > = 2+3+13 = **18 Points**
> > > = 18 Points / 2 Points per Sprint = **9 Sprints**
> > = 4 min + range 5-7 min + range 20-30 min = **29-41**
> **minutes**
> > = range 29-41 min x $1 per min = **$29 - $41**

In practice, the above project estimate can be risk weighted, with additional the estimate being potential the contingency required.

Note: the above is a labour/resource estimation only, it does not include the cost of the actual fruit and required equipment (aka non-resource cost); nor does it include any refrigeration cost (aka ongoing operating expenditure (OPEX)). These are to be added to the above project estimate to obtain a holistic picture of the project budget required.

Some would argue that Agile Estimation is far superior to Absolute Estimation and there are several studies done on this in the Agile community (Agile Alliance, 2015). We have seen many pitfalls and merits to both methods of estimation. Hence, the guidance we provide to projects is if they pick a method of estimation to ensure that this method is based on as much evidence and information as possible at that point in time and a confidence level is set on such an estimate. This will help guide both budgets and forecasts to ensure that implications are captured appropriately in the Cash Flow, Profit & Loss and Balance Sheet.

2.3 Why "Project Cost" can mean different things to different stakeholders?

Most project professionals including Project Managers, Product Owners, Scrum Masters and PMO will think of *Project Cost* as cash outflow (net of any cash inflow i.e. reimbursements) for the Project. There is little consideration given to the Accounting implications of what this cash is being spent on until it is too late.

Accountants explicitly care about implications of cash being spent and the impact it has on the accounting treatments within the Profit & Loss (P&L), Balance Sheet and Cash Flow Statements. The disparity of the different requirements often causes the Project to run into significant financial trouble predominantly due to insufficient P&L allocation (this is unless the organisation is cash-based, rather than accrual-based, and does not care about P&L implications). There have been numerous cases of failed projects and bankrupt organisations in the news over the past 20 years due to this disparity and mismanagement of the longer-term P&L (Bloch, et al., 2012). ***Example 1.5*** illustrates a simple case scenario of project cash and P&L implications.

Example 1.5: A project is looking to spend $100k in cash on procured hardware $50k, software development $40k and travel $10k. What is the Project Cost?

Cash Cost 1st Year:	$'k	P&L Cost 1st Year:	$'k	Comments
Hardware	50	Hardware	-	Hardware is capitalisable and gets depreciated over the useful life of the asset (assume depreciation starts in the 2nd year).
Software Development	40	Software Development	-	Software Development can be capitalisable and gets amortised over the useful life of the asset created (if meets the statutory criteria).
Travel	10	Travel	10	Travel is expensed in the period it is incurred.
Total Cash Cost	100	Total P&L Cost	10	

This example implies that Project Cost means 2 separate answers, but interdependent answers, both of which are correct. The first answer is a Project Cash Cost impact of the project. The second answer is a Project P&L Cost impact of the project and will have an impact for many years to come, which if not accounted for will be an issue for the ongoing investment into future projects.

When setting an estimate or a budget for a project it is **vital** to consider *Project Cost* from both Cash and P&L perspectives across multiple financial years (if this is applicable). This is where the project accounting function brings in value to the organisation. It provides the *translation* mechanism for the project professional's understanding of Project Cost in cash to the accountant's requirements of understanding the P&L implications.

2.4 Introduction to Capitalisation: Is your Project deemed an Asset?

In **Example 1.5**, the reason for the two answers to the question of Project cost is that different components of the Project are deemed either *expensed* or *capitalised*. These are accounting terms used to define whether a component of a project is deemed to impact the P&L immediately (i.e. expensed) or over time (i.e. capitalised and depreciated/amortised over time). This information is very important if a project is funded by an organisation that will have ownership of the project. Ownership and resale value is vital in determining whether a project or a component thereof is *capitalisable. Capitalisation* is an accounting term for creation or recognition of an asset.

Many countries have very different rules around accounting capitalisation. The examples in this book will specifically look at capitalisation rules for projects that fall under the International Financial Reporting Standards (IFRS). This is the most prominent component of a project where Accountants working for your organisation or project must give their professional advice as to whether the project or components thereof are to be considered capitalisable.

Capitalisation is discussed in more depth in **Step 3: Impact: CAPEX and Value** of this book.

2.5 Future Project Implications: Introduction to Benefits and Ongoing Operating Expenses (OPEX)

Future project implications, commonly called benefits, revenue and/or ongoing operating expenses (OPEX) are derived from the Project delivering changes to the client or internal organisation. Most Projects or organisations will have an agreement or mechanism for ensuring that the project implications derived by the project during its delivery timeframe are captured. This is often called *first-year OPEX* and is to be included as part of the Business Case or Lean Canvas.

First-year OPEX is the additional cost that an organisation incurs in the first-year of the project's lifecycle due to the project's deliverable. It is derived due to an action that a project has implemented. This can be the first-year cost of running a software licence to allow the project team to use it to deliver the project itself. This cost must then be included in the organisation's budget in subsequent years, if not done so initially, if this licence will continue to be used by the organisation. The reason behind many projects including this first-year cost as part of its initial project budget is primarily due to budgetary practicality (it is unlikely that any division/team would have spare budget to pay for the first-year OPEX) and secondly to ensure all projects costs are appropriately captured.

Please note that there may be circumstances where first-year OPEX is not captured by the project and are instead captured within the budget of the organisation as a whole. This happens when the project coincides with the budgetary cycle and hence, the organisation can capture this additional cost in the right area of the business to begin with. There may be other reasons why first-year OPEX is not captured by the project, such as reasons of accountability of OPEX in general.

Example 1.6 illustrates a simple case scenario of project cash and P&L implications with first-year OPEX.

There is no standardisation in terminology or delivery approach for future project implications. The reason behind this is the variety of interpretations for project implications in different organisations.

Example 1.6: Using **Example 1.5** as a base case, we also know that to support this project deliverable on an ongoing basis will cost $20k p.a. in OPEX, but will deliver $30k p.a. in new revenue streams. What is the Project Cost?

Cash Cost 1st Year:	$'k	P&L Cost 1st Year:	$'k	Comments
Hardware	50	Hardware	-	
SW Development	40	SW Development	-	If eligible.
Travel	10	Travel	10	
1st Year OPEX	20	1st Year OPEX	20	OPEX is expensed.
Total Cash Cost	**120**	**Total P&L Cost**	**30**	

The additional $30k p.a. revenue stream, which is a benefit derived from the Project is not a Project Cost but is still part of the business case/lean canvas.

The $30k p.a. revenue stream (the benefit), if it is realised during the Project lifecycle, should be recognised by the team that will gain this benefit, rather than the Project i.e. it is not the Project that recognises the revenue stream, but the Division/organisation who ultimately sponsored the project.

When building a software product for an external client, this product will likely generate <u>revenue</u> for your organisation and an <u>OPEX</u> for your client; or if the same software product is built for in-house purposes, this product may generate <u>benefits</u> for one Division and an <u>OPEX</u> for another Division.

No matter the terminology used, many project implications are missed or mismanaged. This happens for several reasons:
- Lack of tracking mechanisms;
- Lack of clear accountability for the project implications; and/or
- Lack of skills or business understanding of implications.

Future project implications are a major part of determining the success or failure of the Project and are a major contributor to various project metrics (discussed below), especially earned value. However, none of the project delivery approaches give clear guidance how to manage these future project implications. This happens due to the Project Manager or Scrum Team moving on to other projects when the Project is considered complete i.e. allocated project spend has occurred and there is no clear guidance who handles ensuring these future project implications are valid and have not eroded throughout time.

The more mature organisations or project delivery environments ensure that the future project implications are handed over to another team before the Project is complete. Usually this is affected most by the changes delivered by the Project. There is nothing stopping the hand-over to be to multiple teams across the organisation. These teams are then ultimately responsible for ensuring that the Project implications are tracked and captured in their ongoing budgets, usually with the help of the Accounting function.

Using forecast or untracked, promised benefit and OPEX profiles delivered by the Project to drive future business budgets can lead to significant repercussions for the future of your organisation. Over-promising and under-delivering to market or shareholder expectations have been a major downfall of many organisations investing in projects.

Future project implications are discussed in more depth in **Step 7: Benefits and OPEX** of this book.

2.6 Contingency and its links to Project Risks & Opportunities

In section *2.2 Original Estimation or Initial Budget*, we briefly mentioned that project contingency is often tagged on to a project due to the inherent uncertainty of the estimation process. Project Managers rarely think through their required contingency post an allocated percentage to the budget. This percentage may be different to the actual risks and opportunities that the project may be facing. This drives two types of behaviours in most organisations or projects:

1. The Executive Board stating that no contingency will be allowed within the project estimation and hence, not accounting for any uncertainties that the project is facing; and/or
2. The Project Managers "hiding" the contingency within their estimation and purposefully over-inflating their required budgets to ensure "adequate" funding in their eyes.

This framework is proposing a different way of dealing with contingency. Rather than putting a blanket percentage on top of required project funding, the Project team should quantify risks and opportunities for the Project during the estimation process. These risks and opportunities require estimation and a probability weighting on the basis of which a contingency can be calculated.

This process allows for traceability and tracking of risks and opportunities, with a quantification attached to them. An example of a way of doing this can be seen in *Example 1.7.*

Example 1.7: Using *Examples 1.5 & 1.6,* here are some risks and opportunities that the Project may face when building an IT solution.

Risk/Opportunity	$'k	% Likelihood	Total $'k
Risk of software development delay by 2 weeks	(6)	50%	(3)
Risk of hardware arrival delay by 4 weeks	(10)	10%	(1)
Opportunity of travel not being required	10	20%	2
Total Contingency Required	**(6)**		**(4)**

The $4k contingency is 3% of the Total Cash Cost of $120k the Project has estimated to spend. The contingency table above may also include a P&L implication column calling out whether there will be additional P&L impact, which helps determine the required P&L for the project. Generally, items that are deemed capitalisable in the estimation will also be capitalisable if contingency is required for these.

2.7 Project Metrics

Many organisations, individuals and published materials will give numerous amounts of project metrics they swear by for calculating whether to invest in a project. However, none guarantee the success of a project. These metrics should be guidelines to test the basic assumptions around the viability of the proposed project only.

It is a good practice to continually reassess these metrics to see whether the assumptions and viability remain within the organisation's interests. This can help drive project prioritisation if there are several projects. Please note, this can be a cumbersome and lengthy exercise to do and is hence, not recommended to be done more than once a quarter (unless there is a delivery approach or business need for it).

This framework provides the most common project metrics used to look at earned value in delivery. It also briefly examines their usefulness for projects and the organisation.

- **Net Present Value** (NPV) is a measure of profitability used in budgeting to assess a given project's potential return on investment (Boyte-White, 2016). All project net cash flows are discounted by a required rate of return or discount rate, which represents the organisation's cost of capital.
  This means that using an interest rate provided by the organisation as a minimum return on investment requires bringing back a calculated NPV > 0. An NPV > 0 will tell the organisation to what extent the project will yield returns above the organisation's required rate of return.

$$PV_{t=0} = \sum_{t=1}^{T} \frac{CF_t}{(1+i)^t}$$

$$NPV = \sum_{t=1}^{T} \frac{CF_t}{(1+i)^t} - CF_0$$

Where:

CF_t = net cash flow during period t

CF_0 = initial investment cost

PV = present value

i = discount rate

t = number of time periods

NPV = net present value

Please note, that an NPV < 0 does not automatically mean the idea for the project will be scrapped. The project may be pursued for other reasons i.e. strategic benefit, social good, compliance and regulation, etc. It will mean that rather than making a potential yield on the project, the organisation will spend more money on the project than it will return.

- **Internal Rate of Return** (IRR) is the metric for the rate of growth the project generates (Investopedia, n.d.). It is the discount rate that brings back the NPV = 0. The formula for this measure is the same as the NPV. Required Rate of Return (RRR) is the minimum annual percentage earned by an investment, which will encourage the Executive Board to invest in a project. This can be a discount rate used to calculate the NVP for a project.

These metrics are often misinterpreted or ignored as many people do not understand them. We recommend that when using these metrics, an explanation what these metrics represent is included for the Executive Board.

- **Weighted Average Cost of Capital** (WACC) is the cost of the organisation's present capital structure (Brown, et al., 2016). All sources of capital are included at a proportional weight.

$$WACC = R_d \times W_d + R_e \times W_e$$
$$WACC = R_d \times \left(\frac{D}{D+E}\right) + R_e \times \left(\frac{E}{D+E}\right)$$

Where:

R_d = After − tax cost of debt capital R_e = Cost of equity capital

D = Market value of debt $\qquad$ W_d = Weighting of debt capital

E = Market value of equity $\qquad$ W_e = Weighting of equity capital

An organisation's WACC is the overall required return. Hence, when decision making around investment in projects is made, this discount rate may be used instead of or in complement to the RRR or IRR.

- **Profitability Index** (PI) (Brown, et al., 2016) is a limited metric used to make quick decisions. When PI > 1, it indicates that the NPV is positive and hence, investment can be made.

$$\text{NPV} = 0, \text{ when } \sum_{t=1}^{T} \frac{CF_t}{(1+i)^t} = CF_0$$

- **Payback period** (Brown, et al., 2016) is the time to break-even on a project investment. This metric does not account for time-value of money, unless a discounted payback period (DPP) is used, where the present value of yearly net cash flows is calculated using a discount rate.

Payback = CF_0 / annual net cash flow

- **Return on Investment** (ROI) is an accounting measure, which is defined by:

ROI = Profit / Project Cost (or Invested Capital)

Profit[5] = Revenue – Expenses
This simple metric does not account for time value of money and should be used in conjunction with other discounted cash flow metrics, such as the NVP and/or DPP.

- **Residual Income** (RI) (aka Economic Value Added) (Brown, et al., 2016) is a complex, yet a most useful metric when looking at project earned value over time. This metric combines accounting measures with discounted cash flow techniques to bring back the expected value of the project.

RI = NOPAT – (WACC × CF_0), where:
Net operating profit after tax (NOPAT) = (Revenue – Cost of Goods Sold – Operating Expenses) x (1 – Tax Rate)

$$\text{Value of Project} = BV_0 + \sum_{t=1}^{T} \frac{RI_t}{(1+i)^t} \text{ if project spans over multiple (t)}$$

years and BV denoted book value of the asset at the time of measurement.

---

[5] Note that Profit in this metric ignores tax and other accounting implications.

Example 1.8: Using **Examples 1.5 & 1.6** data, a project is looking to spend $100k in cash and $20k p.a. on ongoing OPEX, with a delivery of $30k p.a. in a new revenue stream over the next 5 years. Assume that the discount rate is 5%, WACC is 25% & tax rate is 30%.

	$'k	Comments
Project Cash Cost (CF_0)	(120)	Refer to **Example 1.6**
Net cash flow (Yr 1)	30	Revenue minus 1st year OPEX
PV of Year 1 cash flow (i = 5%)	28.57	
Total PVs of Years 1 – 5 cash flows	62.34	Yr 2-5, the PV is on net of revenue & OPEX
NPV after Year 1	(91.43)	
NPV after Year 5	(57.66)	
IRR	22%	Excel calculated metric.

$PI = PV / CF_0$

PI = $62.34k / $120k , post Year 5
PI = 0.52, where a PI < 1 is unacceptable, as it indicates an NPV < 0.

Payback = CF_0 / annual net cash flow
Payback = $120k / $10k, i.e. the net of $30k revenue & $20k OPEX
Payback = 10 years, which indicates a long-term payback (whether this payback is acceptable depends on the strategy of the organisation)
Note: In this example the net cash flow in Yr 1 is ignored for ease of calculation.
ROI = Profit / Project Cost (or Invested Capital)

ROI = $10k / ($120k - $30k) x 100%
ROI = 11.1%, which considered against the WACC of 25% is too low (the desired percentage being the WACC of 25%).

RI = NOPAT – (WACC × CF_0)

RI = $30k x (100% – 30%) + (4 yrs x $10k) x (100% – 30%) – (25% x $120k)
For the purposes of this metric, 1st year OPEX and benefit should be included as part of NOPAT.
RI = $19k
Or
Value of Project = $13.64k, which does not represent as a viable investment.

2.8 Stages or Sprints: When to check in with the Project stakeholders

Different project delivery approaches dictate points when the Project team is required to check-in with its stakeholders. These may be driven by thresholds (*Waterfall Delivery Approach*) or retrospectives (*Agile Delivery Approach*). These check-in points may also have a financial impact on either the funding of the Project or financial implications from the Project.

Agile delivery approach: assuming the Project was deemed capitalisable as a whole, at the end of the Sprint, the Project team realised that the entire Sprint had failed. This will mean that the entire Sprint cannot be capitalised and hence, is expensed through the P&L.

Waterfall delivery approach: at the end of the Stage Boundary (AXELOS Limited, 2014) the Project Manager has realised this Project will cost significantly more than the Business Case. There will be several avenues for the Project Manager, including asking for further funding, cutting scope, etc. This will mean that either funding must be found i.e. borrowing further funds or stopping other projects; or benefits may not be realised to the same extent as before, affecting NPV and project value to the organisation.

These implications must be continuously considered by the Project Managers or Project teams, with the help of Accountants, otherwise the Project or organisation can run into financial trouble.

2.9 Putting together the Initial Financial Plan for the Project

This section gives an example of the components above in the one place, to give basic guidance on what an initial financial plan can look like for a project. This is not a prescriptive method of delivery, however, walks through the various components that should be included as part of initial project planning.

Example 1.9: Building on **Examples 1.5-1.8,** an initial financial plan could look like as follows (reminder that $10k travel costs are expenses in Yr 1):

Category ($'k)	Yr 1	Yr 2	Yr 3	Yr 4	Yr 5	Total
Project Cash Cost	(100)					(100)
1st Year OPEX	(20)					(20)
Total Project Cash Cost* (A)	**(120)**					**(120)**
Hardware Depreciation (5yrs)	(10)	(10)	(10)	(10)	(10)	(50)
SW Dev Amortisation (3yrs)	(13)	(13)	(14)	-	-	(40)
Total Project P&L Cost* (B)	**(53)**	**(23)**	**(24)**	**(10)**	**(10)**	**(120)**
Ongoing OPEX (C)	-	(20)	(20)	(20)	(20)	(80)
Benefits (D)	30	30	30	30	30	150
Total Cash Impact (A+C+D)	**(90)**	**10**	**10**	**10**	**10**	**(50)**
Total P&L Impact	**(23)**	**(13)**	**(14)**	**-**	**-**	**(50)**
NPV (rounded)						($58k)
IRR						22%
PI						0.52
Payback period						10 yrs
ROI						11.1%
RI						$19k

Notice that the Total Project Cash Cost and Total Project P&L Cost equate to the same value, these are just spread over different timeframes to ensure Accounting Standards and Tax Implications are treated equally across all organisations.

KEY TAKEAWAYS

- Both Business Case and Lean Canvas have limitations in use. If a Lean Canvas is chosen as the initial document, the value of the project should be given detailed thought rather than "ballpark" initial estimates. If a Business Case is chosen, being mindful that this should be a living document and ensuring it is not too onerous to update will ensure that it remains applicable to the Project.

- The initial estimate compiled by the Project team will be used as a baseline budget for the project. Making sure this budget is as up-to-date as possible at that point in time will be helpful to the project as changes are required.

- When setting an estimate or a budget for a project it is vital to consider Project Cost from both Cash and P&L perspectives across multiple financial years (if applicable).

- Ownership and resale value is vital in determining whether a project or a component thereof is capitalisable. Capitalisation is an accounting term for creation or recognition of an asset.

- First-year OPEX is the additional cost that an organisation incurs in the first-year of the project's lifecycle due to the project's deliverable. First-year OPEX is to be included in the Business Case or Lean Canvas.

- The Project team should quantify risks and opportunities for the Project during the estimation process. Using probability weighting against these risks and opportunities, the project contingency can be calculated.

- Project metrics should be used in determining whether a project is worth pursuing.

- Checking in with project stakeholders drives better stakeholder management and ensures project finances are managed within an appropriate timeframe.

Step 3: Impact - CAPEX and Value

As part of ***2.4 Introduction to Capitalisation: Is your Project deemed an Asset?***, this framework delved into introducing the accounting concepts of *expense* and *capitalisation.* The reason these concepts are so important to project delivery is that each project has potential regulatory and tax implications to the organisation that owns or benefits from the project. The ultimate question that each Project Board/Sponsor and Accountant must determine with the Project team –

Whether the Project is creating an asset?

Capitalisation is the term used to refer to the recognition or creation of an asset. As an example – by constructing a building, we are creating an asset, therefore; the costs associated with building this asset are *capitalisable.* This is a widely used term around the world and is predominantly used by Accountants to describe various circumstances surrounding asset creation and/or recognition.

There are several accounting and taxation considerations required to be made to answer whether a project or a portion thereof is capitalisable. Most countries have different rules around what project cost can be capitalisable and what the useful life of such assets created should or could be.

This is an important step in this framework where the Project Accountant or someone doing such a function must contribute their expertise. Where such expertise is not available, we recommend that either advice is sought externally to the organisation or the Accountant in the organisation obtains training in the rules and regulations applicable to the Project.

This framework will give guidance, based on IFRS, of the different project lifecycle phases and whether these could be capitalisable or expensed.

Please note there will be circumstances under which:

1. The entire project cannot be capitalised and hence is expensed to begin with. *For example,* the project amount is deemed to be immaterial from the project's point of view.

2. There may be differing taxation and accounting treatment to the same phase or project. *For example,* a decision by the organisation cannot override the existing regulatory and taxation rules.

3. If the project is not tracked properly or adequately, the taxation authority may decline tax incentives or concessions otherwise available to the project. *For example,* time tracking may be required in order to capitalise labour hours.

3.1 Project Lifecycle Phases: Capitalised or Expensed

Refer to *1.1 Project delivery approaches* for a reminder of project delivery approaches. For reduced complexity, together with the Project Board/Sponsor and Project team, the Accountant has determined that the Project as a whole is creating an asset and is therefore capitalisable (under accounting standards driven reporting, i.e. *statutory reporting*).

The delivery approach chosen for the Project will drive the phasing of the Project and whether the phase is capitalisable. Some requirements under Accounting Standards are phase specific, looking at whether a phase of a project is capitalisable within a Project itself. With each phase, there are several general questions the Accountant must ask to determine whether it drives capitalisation:

1. Are there any regulatory or statutory restrictions on the specific Project phase being capitalisable?
2. What is being built during this phase or, if capitalisation is to be determined at the end of the phase, what has been built during this phase?

3. Are labour resources associated with the build of this phase time using a time tracking mechanism that clearly identifies how much time and cost is associated with this build?
4. Is the majority of a particular project phase adding or not adding to the value creation of the project i.e. is there any form of erosion of benefits due to a particular phase?
5. What activities within a particular phase must be expensed under regulatory or statutory guidelines?

In practice, the capitalisation of a Project may look as follows:

Waterfall Delivery Approach Capitalisation

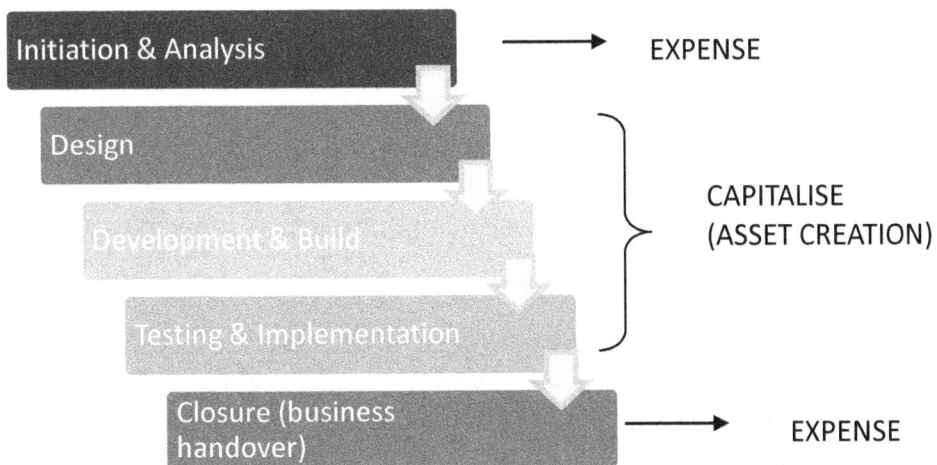

- *Why is 'Initiation' & 'Analysis' not capitalised i.e. an expense?*

According to several Accounting Standards, both Australian and International (i.e. AASB 138, AASB 6, etc.), research and exploration phases are to be expensed. Hence, any phase, regardless of its name that conducts such activities, is to be expensed. The logic behind such a decision is that at this early phase it is unclear whether the Project will go ahead, and it will be almost impossible to tell whether this phase will bring in any benefits. Hence, Accounting Standards take the prudent approach that such activities are not capitalisable.

- *Why is Closure (or maintenance/handover to a Business-as-Usual team) to be expensed?*

  The question of value-add arises for this phase – to what extent is closing off a project contributing to the benefits derived by the project? Generally, the answer is by the end of the previous phase (Implementation) all benefits have been triggered and all that is left over for the Project team to do after Implementation is to document how these benefits are to be tracked by the team(s) to whom hand-over is being delivered. Hence, this phase is deemed in most cases not capitalisable and hence, is expensed.

- *Other activities within the capitalisable phases that should be expensed.*

  As previously mentioned, the Project team should know that there are certain activities that should be expensed as part of capitalised phases (these could differ from country to country and guidance from a local Accountant is required). In Australia, these activities include, but are not limited to travel, entertainment, training, research, change management, etc.

  Again, the general logic behind these is whether the activities are a value-add in building the asset. *For example,* application remediation in software development is an expense, because no additional capability is created. However, if there is any additional application capability or enhancement created which may lead to additional benefits, this type of cost might be capitalisable.

Agile Delivery Approach Capitalisation

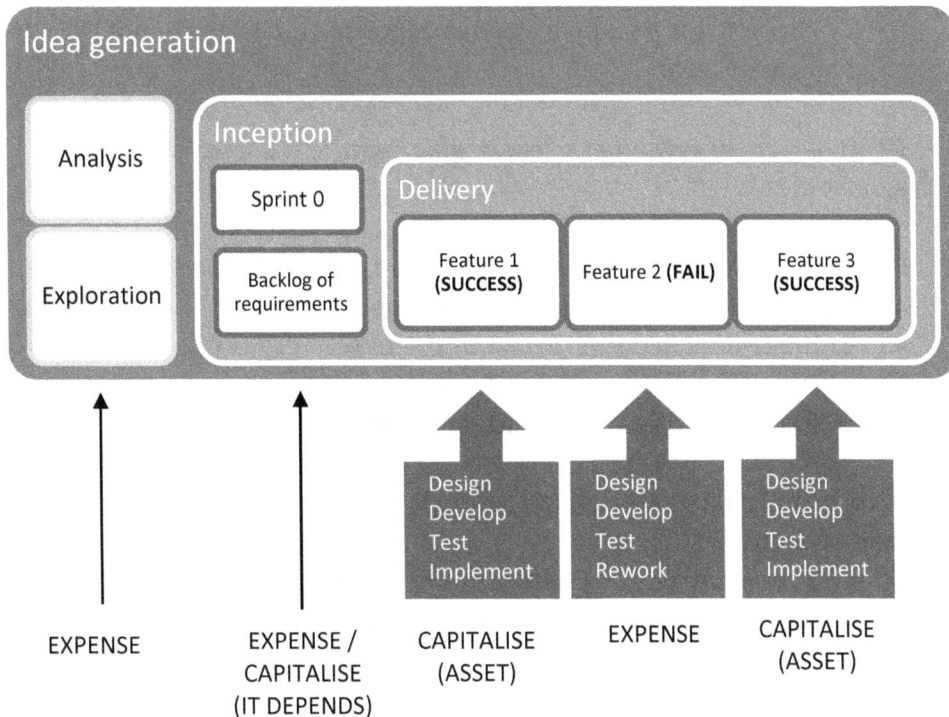

- *Why is Idea generation not capitalised i.e. expensed?*

  Similarly, to the Waterfall Delivery Approach Initiation and Analysis phase, the Idea generation phase is deemed part of the research and exploration phases to be expensed.

- *Why 'Inception' sometimes is expensed and at other times capitalised?*

  Due to the nature of Agile delivery approach, where at the end of each Sprint it is much more transparent as to what has been delivered, it is the recommendation of the this framework to await the completion of each Sprint to determine whether the deliverable is capitalisable. The Inception phase has two components:

  - Sprint 0 – this component could be capitalisable if it is determined to have added value to the overall Project.

- Backlog of requirements – this component is expensed, as even though it is a very important activity to undertake as part of the Project, it is an administrative expense and is hence, not capitalisable.

- *What determines whether a deliverable Feature is capitalisable or expensed?*

  Ultimately whether the Feature developed during one or more Sprints is capitalisable or not depends on its deemed success or failure to value-add to the overall benefits profile of the overall Project being delivered. There are eligibility criteria to be considered as part of this determination specific to Accounting Standards.

  If the Feature fails and requires rework, there are two ways to go about capitalisation:
  1. If the work on the Feature has been capitalised to date, it is the rework component of this Feature that will be expensed. Provided that the Feature will ultimately bring benefits. If the Feature is not reworked and scrapped entirely, then the capitalised work is to be expensed (written-off).
  2. If the work on the Feature has been expensed to date awaiting decision around capitalisation, then capitalisation will only be deemed appropriate once the rework component is complete. Only the portion of the work on the Feature that is deemed to contribute to the Benefits profile will then be capitalised.

- *How is Closure viewed as part of Agile in the context of capitalisation?*

  Agile delivery approach has no formal Closure phase the likes of Waterfall delivery approach. However, the premise of Agile is that as each Feature is completed it is handed over to BAU as a workable, benefits producing component. Materiality of such hand-overs are to be called into question.

  If the Closure of each Feature is a small portion of the overall capitalisable Feature, it is acceptable to have this Closure work remain as part of the capitalisable component of the Feature. However, if the Closure work is complex and hence, requires significant work as part of the Feature's overall work required, then such work must be expensed.

- *Other activities within the capitalisable phases that cannot be capitalised and should be expensed.*

    Please refer to the Waterfall delivery approach comments earlier, surrounding this query.

Note: Without tracking of Project costs, decision making surrounding the above becomes almost impossible. Refer to **Step 6: Systems** for further information.

3.2 Asset creation: Depreciation, Amortisation and Impairment Testing

There is constant debate among organisations as to whether it is better to capitalise or expense projects. Most small-to-medium size organisations do not think about this until it is too late or their project portfolio has become too big to manage as an expense. Often, large-scale projects and organisations may not have a choice and are bound by Accounting Standards and Tax Rules around what can(not) be capitalised and/or expensed.

The main reason behind deciding on project capitalisation, also known as, *asset creation* is that most organisations embarking on either large projects or portfolio of small projects simply do not have enough allocated Profit & Loss budget to invest in such enterprises. Using Accrual Accounting allows for *depreciation & amortisation,* the consequence of which encourages investment and allow for organisations to spread their costs across multiple years.

Depreciation & amortisation is spreading the capitalised project cost across its *useful life.* (Simple way of remembering which is which, *depreciation* is referring to tangible assets and *amortisation* is referring to intangible assets).

Useful life is determined with reference to several Accounting Standards and Guidelines, together with Taxation specific guidelines. These could differ vastly between countries, industries and Taxation entities. Please refer to your local Accountant and Taxation Officer for specific guidelines applicable to your organisation and project.

Once a decision is reached around project capitalisation and its useful life, Accounting Standards may also have rules around *impairment testing. Impairment testing* is thinking about whether the asset is still used and to what extent after project completion. Reduction in derived or expected benefits may also indicate asset impairment. There are very strict guidelines around *impairment testing* of assets set by various Accounting Standards Boards and advice should be sought around your locally applicable rules.

Please refer to *Example 1.9* in **Step 2: Planning** to refresh how this looks in practice.

KEY TAKEAWAYS

- Capitalisation is the term used to refer to the recognition or creation of an asset.

- Most organisations embarking on either large projects or portfolio of small projects simply do not have enough allocated Profit & Loss budget to invest in such enterprises without spreading the cost across multiple years – hence, the reason for capitalisation.

- Expensing or writing off a project cost is to recognise that the cost is incurred in the current financial period rather than deferring out to a future date via the creation of an asset on the Balance Sheet.

- The delivery approach chosen for the Project will drive the phasing of the Project and whether the phase is capitalisable.

- Depreciation & amortisation is spreading the capitalised project cost across its useful life.

    - Depreciation is referring to tangible assets' cost spread across multiple years.

    - Amortisation is referring to intangible assets' cost spread across multiple years.

- Capitalised assets may require impairment testing as to their ongoing carrying value.

Step 4: Workforce Management

As noted in **Step 3: Impact: CAPEX and Value,** to understand what the Project budget has been spent on, a tracking mechanism should be established within the organisation. When referring to tracking of workforce resources i.e. labour cost, this framework refers to this tracking mechanism as *Project Workforce Management*.

The Time Sheet Debate

"You should track your time even if it's just for yourself,
If you do, you will certainly be surprised."
- Stephen Covey, *The 7 Habits of Highly Effective People.*

There has been much debate around whether this step is required and how to best manage project labour in the fast-paced environment we live in today. This framework looks at best practice across multiple industries and subscribes to the view that time should be tracked. The way it is tracked is dependent on what this information is then used for. In practice, the resource management process should be as simple as possible to ensure that the data that is gathered through this process is helpful to the overall Project and does not hinder progress with overly cumbersome requirements.

Project Workforce Management includes a structure set up to track labour cost. For this structure to be appropriately integrated with organisational policy and procedures, the Finance team, generally together with Human Resources, must develop processes and policy in dealing with the following:

- *Project role types* – for simplification and confidentiality purposes, labour resource roles should be grouped into general types i.e. designers, developers, architects, etc. Depending on the size of the labour resource pool, these could be fairly large or small groups of people. The key here is to enable high-level differentiation without layers of complexity when a Project team is required to put together a budget with the labour resources required.

- **Project carded rates** – each Role Type must have a monetary rate assigned i.e. all Designers will cost $1,000 per day to the Project. Again, this is for both simplification and confidentiality purposes. There are several methods in practice to calculate carded rates. The method chosen is largely driven by the need for the *recovery of costs*. This will be discussed further in this book under the section **4.1 Project Carded Rates.**

- **Effort hours charged & measured** – agreement from the Project, HR and Finance must be reached regarding this component as this becomes a contentious issue in practice. How many hours may be charged to the Project? How are these hours to be measured? What is deemed to be a "productive hour"? These are all questions this book will work through to provide practical examples under the section **4.2 Effort Hours Charged & Measured.**

- **KPI output** – in many organisations labour resources will likely work on multiple projects simultaneously and might have BAU work. Ultimately, Key Performance Indicators (KPIs) for labour resources must be set in such a way as to drive performance[6].

- **Time sheeting / tracking** – to enable the components of this framework to work in the most optimum manner, the organisation must decide on a mechanism to track time. The driving force behind this activity must be the Executive Board as only management can set this prerequisite. This will be discussed further in this book under the section **4.3 Time Tracking.**

- **Scheduling** – this activity is historically done as part of Waterfall Delivery Approach, where a (Project or Portfolio) Scheduler will look at compiling when the work should be done and ensure that resources are made available. Scheduling is also often used to sequence projects,

---

[6] Please refer to http://davidparmenter.com for further information.

especially when resources and projects overlap during the same timeframes and deliverables. The larger the organisation, the more complex this activity becomes, with multiple Schedulers and teams thereof. This framework strongly recommends investing in Scheduling resources both human and software tools to allow for proper optimisation of labour regardless of project delivery approach chosen.

- **Skills-based subdivision** – rather than splitting by role type, some organisational structures split teams by skill sets, these can be Value Streams or Platforms. This is argued to be conducive of enabling a more agile working environment. Splitting teams by skill sets can be quite a complex exercise, especially in existing organisations for whom the concept is new.

  However, the key here is to ensure clear team structures are set without overcomplicated matrix structures enabling a clearer cross-functional agile working environment.

4.1 Project Carded Rates

These rates are often called *charge out rates* – the rate at which a labour resource charges their time to the Project. The main reasons behind these rates are confidentiality of salary disclosures and ease of forecasting/budgeting project cost with relatively simple calculations.

Each organisation comes up with its own ways of calculating carded rates, noting these calculations are often similar to the way someone would price their time in the Advisory/Consulting industry or how a product would be priced. The concept of *recovery of costs* is the key to these calculations. *Recovery of costs* is how much of the cost incurred is to be recovered from the Project, client or customer.

Example 2.0 shows a simplistic way of working out the carded rate for a specific team. There are several components that each organisation requires to decide on when compiling carded rates:

- What types of costs are to be included in the carded rates? – These can range from salaries only to a broad range of associated staff on-costs related to assumed productivity, etc.
  NB. Care must be taken to ensure that this is then appropriately reflecting when making capitalisation decisions.
- How many days does the organisation assume for the team? – Some projects may work 365 a year and have expected shift work.
- What happens when staff leave and may not be replaced? – this requires consideration for *over/under recovery of cost* i.e. a team may make a profit or loss due to staff leaving or being replaced by more expensive/cheaper labour. Some organisations do what is known as a *true-up* of cost on a quarterly basis. A *true-up* of costs is referring to an accounting "clean-up" of any profit or loss made from *over/under recovery of cost* in the specific team. This may require a revision of carded rates (this is generally quite a costly exercise and is not done often i.e. bi-annually/annually).
- Some labour resources may have flexible arrangements i.e. part-time – these arrangements are also required to be considered when calculating carded rates, especially if there is a material impact.

Example 2.0: To work out the Carded Rate of Team A below, which has 10 labour resources, we look at the following costs associated with this team:

Cost	Value	Comments
Base Salaries	$1,000,000	average $100k p.a.
Salary on-cost	$95,000	i.e. superannuation/pension contribution
Total	**$1,095,000**	**Cost per annum**
Divide by	10	labour resources
Divide by	260	working days p.a.
Carded Rate	**$421**	**per day per labour resource in Team A**

Ultimately, the meaning of the above Carded Rate is that in order to recover the cost of Team A, the Project (and the client) must as a minimum be charged at the above rate i.e. to break even.

From these considerations, the question arises whether carded rates are still worth the hassle considering the complexity around calculating these rates. The way to look at carded rates is how organisations look at pricing their products and/or services. Just as material underlying changes to the cost of production of a product will mean that an organisation will pass on any price changes to their customers, so too is the idea of carded rates. This is not an exercise that is done often, however, it is vital to understand the true cost of the Project.

4.2 Effort Hours Charged & Measured

To achieve simplicity in both systems and ways of working when looking at project cost, an agreement must be reached between the Project team(s), HR and Finance regarding the assumed working hours of each labour resource. In *Example 2.0*, the card rate calculated was a daily rate for simplicity. However, many employee contracts have a minimum and/or maximum daily hour limit that an employee must work. This becomes important when calculating budgets for shift and weekend work, contractors and flexible employees.

In practice, contracts are often ignored for ease of budgeting / forecasting purposes and the Project assumes that labour resources work 7.5-9 hours per day. From a materiality perspective, this is seen to be the norm and will only make a significant difference to project cost if labour resources are getting paid for significant after-hours work. Some organisations with internal projects will cap the chargeable working hours to projects i.e. any time a labour resource works outside the assumed hours of work, these will either be deemed as non-chargeable hours; a cost to their Team cost centre; or will be enforced as time-in-lieu.

4.3 Time Tracking

There are many arguments pro and against time tracking or time sheeting for projects. Regardless of whether someone agrees with doing it or not, very strong opinions are on the matter. Many arguments against time tracking stem from the notion that by doing so, there will be dire consequences to the individual. In his article "Why Project Accounting?" Finch (2007)[7], provides these reasons to resist time tracking:

1. Reporting time seems to threaten status i.e. an Executive filling in a timesheet can feel demoted.
2. "What if I find out that I don't work as much as I like to think?" – The thought of finding out the truth about what we spend time on is scary.
3. Time is a bad metric for effort of productivity i.e. time spent is not a metric for productivity, however, it helps understand the efficiency at which something is produced. This Is especially important as a project moves into an Agile delivery approach environment.
4. "I'm too busy" gets cited every time employees with the highest demand on their time must fill in timesheets are requested to do so. With today's variety of tracking software, applications and automation, surely this cannot still be an excuse, but it is the most widely and most commonly used excuse.

Unfortunately, without adequate time tracking there is no way to truly tell the project cost or the efficiency of the labour resources completing the scheduled tasks. Insufficient time tracking ultimately leads to "bad project accounting... [where] bad project accounting leads to unnecessary overtime; stressful, blown schedules; bad estimates; and cancelled projects." There are many benefits of project time tracking, which outweigh the minor nuisance of completing a timesheet:

1. Priceless data, which allows for understanding the cost of the project so it can be used for decision making presently and in the future.
2. If insufficiently or inappropriately tracked, the definition and hence, benefits of capitalisation, as discussed in **Step 3: Impact: CAPEX and Value** cannot be taken advantage of.

---

[7] Copyright 2007 by IMA®, Montvale, N.J., www.imanet.org, used with permission.

3. There are several potential tax incentives, concessions and programs that a Project or organisation could qualify for provided that evidence such as time sheeting is presented.

Finch (2007) notes that time tracking is Project Accounting's Achilles' heel, as the entire field relies on data collection. The data collected is essentially what drives decision making on whether to "stop, start, continue" (Williams, 2014) an activity or Project. If the data relied upon is "rubbish", then as they say – "rubbish in, rubbish out".

KEY TAKEAWAYS

- Project Workforce Management includes a structure to track labour cost.

- Project Workforce Management must give (Business Dictionary, n.d.) consideration to:

  1. Project role types
  2. Project carded rates
  3. Effort hours charged & measured
  4. KPI output
  5. Time sheeting / tracking
  6. Scheduling
  7. Skills-based subdivision

- Time needs to be tracked in order to capture project value.

- Time tracking must be driven as a practice by the Executive Board.

- Among other reasons, the argument for time tracking is that it is used for supporting capitalisation.

Step 5: Tracking

At this stage of the framework, all the surrounding organisational project policies and procedures would have been set up. Please refer to **Steps 1-4** to recap the procedural and policy requirements to allow for the project to reach this stage. In this Step, the project is now active and is delivering the required project scope. Once the project has started its deliverables, most of the Project Accountant's time will be spent on these activities:

1.1 Completing ongoing rolling forecasts
1.2 Fitting the project timeframes and deliverables into the Accounting cycles
1.3 Variance analysis and insights
1.4 Earned value analysis and KPI output
1.5 Modelling scenario analysis
1.6 Contingency tracking and financial risk mitigation

5.1 Completing ongoing rolling forecasts

Why? Projects by their nature are not business as usual (BAU) activities, where deliverables and expenses are the same monthly, with minimal changes. Projects are generally investment activities, which involve timeframes where expenses and deliverables differ from month-to-month (or Sprint-to-Sprint). Hence, unlike the BAU activities historically forecast or re-budgeted, projects and portfolios thereof require to be tracked monthly, or Sprint basis, also referred to in Accounting as a *rolling forecast.*

Who? Depending on the size, materiality and risk of the Project, the Project Accountant will work with the Project team, usually the Project Manager or Scrum Master/Product Owner, to determine the deliverables, whether draft or concrete for the next month, Sprint, quarter, year, etc. These deliverables will drive forecast cost as each deliverable will likely have both/either labour resource and non-resource costs associated with it.

How? The Project Accountant will then help the Project team represent this information (using a form of software or templates discussed in **Step 6: Systems**) to facilitate decision making for both the Accounting Division and Project Board/Sponsor.

Please see ***Example 2.1*** for a brief example of what an ongoing rolling forecast looks like.

There is much debate in the Accounting community whether quarterly rolling forecasts that are used for BAU activities are sufficient for project forecasting. Based on industry experience, this framework is of the view that quarterly rolling forecasts are insufficient in the Project world. Projects work in shorter and significant intervals and hence, monthly rolling forecasts are required at a minimum to drive appropriate decision making. Note, also that *agile delivery approach* Sprint drivers that may be shorter cycles than monthly may require the rolling forecast to be more frequent which may lead to significant project implications.

Example 2.1:

The following is an example of a rolling forecast that allows for variance analysis for a 2-month project.

EAC is an industry acronym used for Estimate at Completion and signifies how much the project is looking to spend at a point in time overall and *WD* denotes work day.

Please note, most data will not be available more frequently than monthly, as most organisations either have monthly billing cycles i.e. bills get paid once a month, not as they come in or time sheeting does not get completed as the work is done, but rather once a month as it is due.

May-01 EAC

Resources	Team	Rate (per day)	May-01 F'cast (WD)	May-01 F'cast ($)	Jun-01 F'cast (WD)	Jun-01 F'cast ($)	Total EAC (WD)	Total EAC ($)
John Smith	Team A	$1,000	10	$10,000	20	$20,000	30	$30,000
Alec Bald	Team B	$500	20	$10,000	20	$10,000	40	$20,000
Fiona Mac	Team A	$1,000	5	$5,000	-	-	5	$5,000
Raj Man	Team C	$750	10	$7,500	20	$15,000	30	$22,500
Non-Resources								
Hardware				$10,000		-		$10,000
Total				$42,500		$45,000		**$87,500**

The above project forecast for a 2-month project is forecasting to spend $87,500. In practice, this initial forecast will also be the project budget. The Project Accountant will take this to the Accounting Division to ensure that appropriate investment funding is allocated.

Example 2.1 (continued):

Let's have a look at one month into the project what happens:

May-01 Actual Cost

Resources	Team	Rate (per day)	May-01 Actual (WD)	May-01 Actual ($)	May-01 F'cast (WD)	May-01 F'cast ($)	Var. (WD)	May-01 Var. ($)
John Smith	Team A	$1,000	5	$5,000	10	$10,000	5	$5,000
Alec Bald	Team B	$500	10	$5,000	20	$10,000	10	$5,000
Fiona Mac	Team A	$1,000	5	$5,000	5	$5,000	-	-
Raj Man	Team C	$750	15	$11,250	10	$7,500	(5)	($3,750)
Non-Resources								
Hardware				-		$10,000		$10,000
Total				$26,250		$42,500		**$16,250**

The above results suggest several factors may have taken place such as:
- Potential slow ramp-up of certain project activities;
- Labour resources (not) required to the same extent as originally forecast;
- Labour resources potentially not completing timesheets; and
- Hardware not arriving on time and hence, no accrual or payment has taken place.

Only by reviewing the above costs monthly, together with the Project team, the Project Accountant can help determine an appropriate latest forecast.

Example 2.1 (continued):

Assuming the following circumstances occurred in May-01 that we have discovered from our conversations with the Project team, this is what the rolling forecast will then look like for the 2-month project:

- Team A has completed their work in a shorter period and hence, have not charged the full amount of time originally forecast – this is known as a *permanent variance;*
- Team B was slow to ramp up and is yet to complete the work required. To complete the work on time, they will need to provide an extra resource in Jun-YY – this is known as a *timing variance;*
- Team C has completed their work, however, due to unforeseen issues has required putting in more days than originally forecast – this is known as a *permanent variance.*

The hardware has not arrived as originally forecast and as per Accounting Standards cannot be accrued for – this is known as a *timing variance.*

Hence, the overall $16,250 variance for the month of May-01 can be split into two parts:

- *Permanent variance* = Team A $5,000 variance - Team C $3,750 variance = $1,250 is a permanent saving to the project and is NOT to be added to the rolling forecast.
- *Timing variance* = Team B $5,000 variance + Hardware $10,000 variance = $15,000 is a timing variance and hence needs to be added back into the rolling forecast.

Example 2.1 (continued):

Jun-01 EAC

Resources	Team	Rate (per day)	May-01 Actual (WD)	May-01 Actual ($)	Jun-01 F'cast (WD)	Jun-01 F'cast ($)	Total EAC (WD)	Total EAC ($)
John Smith	Team A	$1,000	5	$5,000	20	$20,000	25	$25,000
Alec Bald	Team B	$500	10	$5,000	20	$10,000	30	$15,000
Fiona Mac	Team A	$1,000	5	$5,000	-	-	5	$5,000
Raj Man	Team C	$750	15	$11,250	20	$15,000	25	$26,250
Max Payne	Team B	$500	-	-	10	$5,000	10	$5,000
Non-Resources								
Hardware				-		$10,000		$10,000
Total				$26,250		$60,000		**$86,250**

As noted, the new forecast to completion (FTC) reflects the permanent variance of $1,250 only to ensure that forecast (budget) for the remaining aspects of the project is not lost.

5.2 Fitting the Project timeframes and deliverables into the Accounting cycles

Why? The challenge and goal for the Executive Board, Project team and Project Accountant is to ensure that the project(s) fit within the Accounting cycles and project delivery timeframes alike. This is mainly because most organisations still work on yearly budgeting cycles, which are inappropriate for the Project industry. Projects will encounter a fine balancing act illustrated by the Golden Triangle of Quality, Schedule and Budget (Warner, 2017), where all of these will need to be accommodated for within the Accounting cycles.

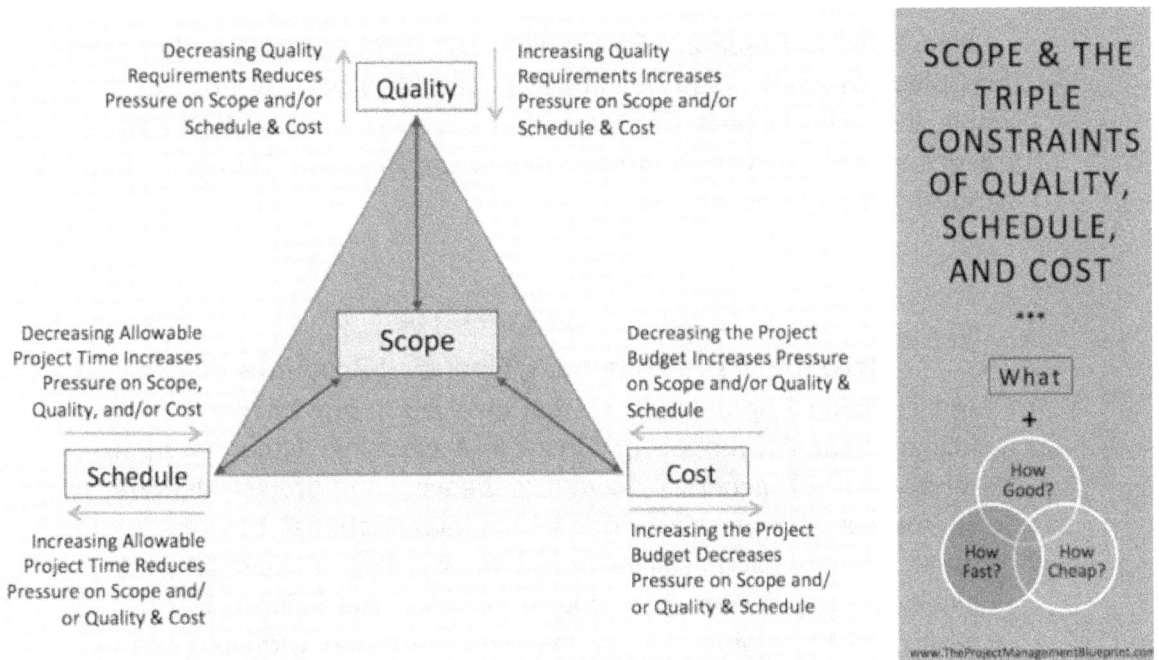

Decreasing Quality Requirements Reduces Pressure on Scope and/or Schedule & Cost

Quality

Increasing Quality Requirements Increases Pressure on Scope and/or Schedule & Cost

Scope

Decreasing Allowable Project Time Increases Pressure on Scope, Quality, and/or Cost

Decreasing the Project Budget Increases Pressure on Scope and/or Quality & Schedule

Schedule

Cost

Increasing Allowable Project Time Reduces Pressure on Scope and/ or Quality & Cost

Increasing the Project Budget Decreases Pressure on Scope and/ or Quality & Schedule

SCOPE & THE TRIPLE CONSTRAINTS OF QUALITY, SCHEDULE, AND COST

...

What

+

How Good?

How Fast?

How Cheap?

www.TheProjectManagementBlueprint.com

Source: *Scope and the Golden Triangle of Quality, Schedule, & Budget* (Warner, 2017) [8]

Who? Depending on the size, materiality and risk of the Project, the Project Accountant will work with the Project team, usually the Project Manager or Scrum Master/Product Owner and the Accounting Division to ensure that where any of the above Golden Triangle attributes are

---

[8] Scope and the Golden Triangle of Quality, Schedule, & Budget ©, 2017, Mark Warner. Reproduced with permission.

impacted this will be included in financial forecasts. The earlier the determination of any material changes in forecast, the earlier the Executive Board and the Accounting Division can decide around the continuation of the project and its required resource/funding allocations.

How? The Project Accountant will continuously work with the Project team to ensure that the significant deviations from the Golden Triangle (Warner, 2017) are represented appropriately within financial Quarterly/Bi-annual/Yearly forecasts and budgets giving clarity on where the project(s) are placed at that stage in time.

Please see *Example 2.2* for an example of the interaction between the Golden Triangle attributes and Accounting cycles. To illustrate this simple example, project delivery approach is irrelevant. However, in practice project delivery approach will likely drive the Golden Triangle attributes in a significant way.

Project Accountant vs
Traditional (Management/Financial) Accountant

The Traditional Accountant is often involved in one of two roles – Management Accounting or Financial Accounting. Either or both roles DO NOT generally have experience with project delivery approaches. These roles work within organisational business-as-usual activities, and usually lack understanding of how to track and/or account for projects. Due to major project failures over the past 20 years, mainly due to the misunderstanding of long-term financial implications of projects, the Project Accountant's role has been to proactively help the Traditional Accountant and Project Sponsor to ensure that projects are accounted for properly.

Example 2.2:

Using a similar example to ***Example 2.1*** please note the additional information:

- The organisation has a financial year end in June of each year.
- Originally the 2-month project was to span over the single financial year cycle i.e. May & June of the same financial year.
- The approved project budget of $87,500 was for the single financial year.
- Accounting policy states that budget is approved for one financial year at a time.
- Assume all costs are material to the organisation.

May-01 EAC

Resources	Team	May-01 F'cast ($)	Jun-01 F'cast ($)	Total FY01 EAC ($)
John Smith	Team A	$10,000	$20,000	$30,000
Alec Bald	Team B	$10,000	$10,000	$20,000
Fiona Mac	Team A	$5,000	-	$5,000
Raj Man	Team C	$7,500	$15,000	$22,500
Non-Resources				
Hardware		$10,000	-	$10,000
Total		$42,500	$45,000	**$87,500**

As per ***Example 2.1***, the project experienced certain delays due to Team B in the month of May. Unfortunately, unlike in ***Example 2.1,*** in this example, Team B was unable to allocate an additional labour resource for the month of June.

The project has a few different options according to the Golden Triangle, each with material impacts to the project:

- **Scenario 1:** The Project team can choose not to complete the work that Team B was expected to complete, therefore potentially decreasing *Quality & Scope,* not increasing overall *Cost* by $5,000 for Max Payne (refer to ***Example 2.1***) and having *Schedule* stay the same.

Example 2.2 (continued):

- **Scenario 2:** The Project team can choose to extend its *Schedule* to next financial year and assuming Team B is available, bring in the extra resource to finish the work. Thereby delaying the *Schedule* of the project, not compromising on the *Quality,* but will now encounter the circumstance where the project budget will need to be requested in order to increase *Cost* and move budget into the next financial year.

Assuming that the Project team has chosen **Scenario 2** whereby the requirement is to move project budget between financial years. The tables below illustrate what this will look like from an accounting point of view whether there is project accounting involvement or not.

Under the circumstances where there is NO Project Accountant involved with helping the Project team i.e. a Traditional (Management/Financial) Accountant is involved only:

Jun-01 EAC (NO Project Accountant)

Resources	Team	May-01 Actual ($)	Jun-01 F'cast ($)	Total FY01 EAC ($)	Jul-02 F'cast ($)	Total FY02 EAC	Total Project EAC
John Smith	Team A	$5,000	$20,000	$25,000	-	-	$25,000
Alec Bald	Team B	$5,000	$10,000	$15,000	-	-	$15,000
Fiona Mac	Team A	$5,000	-	$5,000	-	-	$5,000
Raj Man	Team C	$11,250	$15,000	$26,250	-	-	$26,250
Non-Resources							
Hardware		-	-	-	-	-	-
Total		$26,250	$45,000	**$71,250**	-	-	**$71,250**

Notes:

- Due to Quarterly forecasting, which would have been done in Mar-01 or Apr-01, the Traditional Accountant will miss out on all the *rolling forecast* changes discussed in **Example 2.1**;
- the Traditional Accountant will miss out on all the *rolling forecast* changes discussed in **Example 2.1**;

Example 2.2 (continued):

- The Traditional Accountant will report the project forecast to be $71,250, which will then cause an unexpected "surprise" when the project will come in at potentially $15,000 higher than expected, assuming the hardware accrual is missed.

In this case, it is also very unlikely for the project to gain the budget to continue into FY02, as budgets would have been finalised by this stage and any continuation would jeopardise the other projects whose budget has been factored into the following financial year.

Under the circumstances where there is a Project Accountant involved with helping the Project team (using the Actual cost from *Example 2.1*):

Jun-01 EAC (WITH Project Accountant)

Resources	Team	May-01 Actual ($)	Jun-01 F'cast ($)	Total FY01 EAC ($)	Jul-02 F'cast ($)	Total FY02 EAC	Total Project EAC
John Smith	Team A	$5,000	$20,000	$25,000	-	-	$25,000
Alec Bald	Team B	$5,000	$10,000	$15,000	$5,000	$5,000	$20,000
Fiona Mac	Team A	$5,000	-	$5,000	-	-	$5,000
Raj Man	Team C	$11,250	$15,000	$26,250	-	-	$26,250
Non-Resources							
Hardware		-	$10,000	$10,000	-	-	$10,000
Total		$26,250	$55,000	**$81,250**	$5,000	**$5,000**	**$86,250**

Notes:

- The *rolling forecast* changes discussed in *Example 2.1* are captured i.e. the $10k for hardware doesn't disappear;
- The Total Project EAC is the same as discussed in *Example 2.1;*
- In this case, it is very likely that the project will be allowed to be completed in FY02, as this impact will be delivered to both the Accounting Division and Executive Board in a timely manner by the Project Accountant and will allow for proper management of budgeted funds for FY02.

5.3 Variance Analysis and Insights

Why? One of the key reasons behind *rolling forecasts* is the ability to analyse the financial variances on an ongoing basis (which also drive **5.4 Earned value analysis and KPI output** discussed in the next section). This variance analysis provides key insights into how the project is tracking financially and ensuring that project budget remains valid.

Who? Depending on the size, materiality and risk of the Project, the Project Accountant will work with the Project team, usually the Project Manager or Scrum Master/Product Owner, to work through the implications of the monthly variance analysis. For this exercise to add value to both the Project team and the organisation, this framework advises these conversations consider *materiality* (i.e. significance of the variances to the organisation). Where variances are *immaterial* to the Project or the organisation, this framework recommends bringing the conversation to a higher-level grouping of variances in a logical way.

Materiality for projects is different for every organisation and is often driven by the Executive Board and/or the Accounting Division.

How? Each month the Project Accountant will compile the actual costs for the month from the Accounting General Ledger and compare these with the forecast locked in with the Project team for the month before. The variance between the actual cost and the forecast cost is the *variance analysis.* Through variance analysis, the Project Accountant will provide insights into the material variances by calling out *permanent* and *timing variances* much like in **Example 2.1.** These insights are important in ensuring timely decision making related to the project. For example, a massive cost blow-out due to unforeseen circumstances in a project may leave a severe funding gap, which the organisation must somehow close to continue with the project scope.

5.4 Earned value analysis and KPI output

Why? Cost variance analysis and provision of monthly/quarterly/Sprint insights will not be enough to truly understand how the project is tracking compared with scope and schedule. This is where earned value analysis (EVA) comes in to determine whether completion of project milestones or Sprints corresponds to expected spend.

Who? This framework recommends that an EVA is done for *material* or significant projects only, as this can be a time consuming and onerous exercise. An EVA is compiled by a Project Accountant, as an impartial party, with the inputs from the Project team and accounting systems. If a Project Accountant is not available to compile such an analysis, this framework recommends using an impartial Business Analyst and/or Accountant not reporting to the Project team to ensure that data integrity remains.

Materiality for projects is different for every organisation and is often driven by the Executive Board and/or the Accounting Division.

How? Each month the Project Accountant will refer to data provided by the PMO, Scheduler, Wall or Project team to compile % complete. The actual costs will be taken from the Accounting General Ledger, and prior month and budget comparisons will be included in order for the analysis to be conducted, as per *Example 2.3*.

Example 2.3:

Using **Examples 2.1 & 2.2** at Jun-01 EAC, the following EVA was conducted with the help of the Project team.

Note: the following table assumes that each Team has its own deliverable milestone; this is done for ease of comparison of this example only. In practice, the project will generally have Sprints or Milestones, where teams will achieve by working cross-functionally or as waterfall delivery.

Example 2.3:

EVA	Actual to May-01	Forecast to May-01	EAC (c)	Budget (d)	%Actual EAC	%F'cast Budget	% Complete (per schedule)
	(a)	(b)	(c)	(d)	(a) / (c)	(b) / (d)	
Team A	$10,000	$15,000	$30,000	$35,000	33%	43%	43%
Team B	$5,000	$10,000	$20,000	$20,000	25%	50%	25%
Team C	$11,250	$7,500	$26,250	$22,500	43%	33%	33%
HW	-	$10,000	$10,000	$10,000	-	100%	-
Total	$26,250	$42,500	$86,250	$87,500	30%	49%	~35%

The "so what"?

Provided an EVA is compiled in a timely manner, it will provide the answers to the key project question – the "so what"?

- *% Actual to EAC*: this metric represents the actual cost to date divided by the current month's Estimate at Completion (EAC) (aka how much the project is tracking to cost overall at a point in time).

- *% Forecast to Budget / prior month EAC*: this metric should be divided into 2 separate metrics in following the month of May-01 - *% Forecast to Budget* and *% Forecast to prior month EAC.* This metric represents the expected spend for the current month compared to both budget and prior month's EAC.

- *% Complete (per Schedule)*: this metric is generally taken from either the latest project schedule or Wall (agile delivery approach). At times, this is a difficult metric to gain access to, as the Project team will find it tempting to align their achievement with the project spend.

Practical Tip: In practice, it is advisable to gain the *% Complete* metric first, before looking at the cost and expected cost for the month. This way it does not allow for questioning the heuristic until all data is compiled together.

Example 2.3 (continued):

So what?

1. The 30% actual to EAC is saying that the project has currently spent 30% of its EAC by the end of May-01.
    Since the data is only for one month, we can compare this with the next column of % Forecast to Budget (which is also the expected spend for the project to date).
2. Here we can see that the project has under spent significantly compared with the expected 49% spend for the project to date.
    These 2 points of information are known to us from the insights previously presented in *Example 2.1.* However, the 3rd point below is the additional unknown.
3. The Scheduler has indicated, that in fact the % complete for the project is ~35% as at the end of May-01.
4. When compared with the 30% actual to EAC and 49% forecast to budget, the % complete of ~35% is showing that the project is likely to under spend, however, looks to potentially not meet its current project schedule either.

Overall, an EVA provides an overall picture of comparative information in the one place, which can be presented as a dashboard for the Project Board/Sponsor and Executive Board.

Note: In practice, an EVA is rarely done by many organisations or projects. The main reason behind this is that most Project Boards/Sponsors and/or Executive Boards do not understand the analysis provided and are often too time poor to invest in understanding this analysis. Hence, if an EVA is embarked upon, we suggest making it as interactive and easy to read as possible, using dashboards and colours to signify areas that require the Project Boards/Sponsors and/or Executive Board's attention.

5.5 Modelling Scenario Analysis

Why? Project teams and Project Boards/Sponsors often must make crucial decisions as to which course of action to take in various scenarios. Simulations and scenario analysis modelling can help facilitate decision making and manage risk. Detailed scenario analysis often happens at three crucial points in time:

1. Prior to gaining approval for the project budget;
2. In Waterfall delivery approach, between Stages or prior to moving on to the next Stage; or/and
3. In Agile delivery approach, when allocated funding has run out and continuation of the project is analysed as a possibility.

Who? In practice, this activity is often done by a Business Analyst with the guidance of a Project Accountant on the Accounting implications to the organisation and project. However, Project Accountants have the skills to complete this analysis.

How? There are many professional techniques such as the Monte Carlo or What-if analysis, appropriate to project modelling scenario analysis. Risk weighting comes into many scenario analyses, which is important to capture as part of the project risks and contingency (if applicable). This framework will not expand on these techniques. These are mentioned here as available techniques which may require further research into financial modelling if these techniques are deemed appropriate.

5.6 Contingency tracking and financial risk mitigation

Why? As noted in section **2.6 Contingency and its links to Project Risks & Opportunities,** risks and opportunities should be attached to contingency to quantify how much contingency is required. These risks and opportunities then need to be continuously tracked through a process of *contingency management*. As risks and opportunities are realised, a contingency may have to be drawn upon or released. Mismanagement of contingency may lead to a complete loss in confidence in the project's management. Hence, transparency of how contingency is being used by a project can lead to confidence in the proper management of the project.

Who? This activity is done by either the Project team or Project Accountant if done. In practice, contingency management is done for either material projects or large portfolios of projects where contingency is allocated as a pool to be drawn upon. This task can get complex over time, hence, an adequate approvals process using the Executive Board is very important to ensure transparency.

How? Please refer to **Example 1.7** as a basis of how contingency can be managed. This example shows a simple template that can be used in contingency management.

KEY TAKEAWAYS

- The following activities make up the main responsibilities of a Project Accountant's role:
    - Completing ongoing rolling forecasts
    - Fitting the project timeframes and deliverables into the Accounting cycles
    - Variance analysis and insights
    - Earned value analysis and KPI output
    - Modelling scenario analysis
    - Contingency tracking and financial risk mitigation

- Ongoing (monthly) project forecasts are required to help drive decision-making as to the potential estimate at completion of a project.
  Practical Tip: These are generally completed just before month-end closure, to ensure the smooth closure of month-end reporting.

- Project teams often do not realise that project timeframe deliverables need to correspond to the existing financial year within which a budget is approved and therefore risk losing their budget.

- Variance analysis helps ensure that permanent and timing differences in cost are captured appropriately in forecast and EAC. So that the project does not "lose" its budget just because of a monthly (timing) underspend.

- If used, an earned value analysis can provide a holistic project financial update that can help decision making.

- Contingency management is ensuring that as risks and opportunities are realised, a contingency is drawn upon or released. Mismanagement of contingency may lead to a loss in confidence of the project's management.

Step 6: Systems

Throughout **Steps 1-5,** this framework briefly mentions the use of the General Ledger to access the actual costs for project(s). This implies that organisations have accounting systems in place to track costs. However, this does not mean that these accounting systems are integrated with other organisational systems in place to optimise the use of the data. This Step concentrates on financial tracking consistency and how to ensure that all financial results for a project are reported in a consistent and transparent manner.

It may come as a surprise to many non-finance professionals that when asking for numbers from the Accounting Division, you may end up with a different answer depending on the day of the week or month this question is asked. This is mainly due to system integration and update cycles at which Accountants work. Please see *Example 2.4* for an example.

Example 2.4: If you were to ask your Accountant for the actual results for your project at month-end, you will get a completely different result than if you were to ask for the same results at any other given day of that month. This is not because the numbers are wrong, but because they are generally incomplete, as the Accountant is working away at ensuring that payments are made and accruals are raised. All of this gets finalised for the month by month-end.

Accountants, as noted previously, work within a General Ledger – a database that holds a complete record of financial transactions over the life of the organisation. The General Ledger may be a simple spreadsheet or a complex system that integrates with several other organisational systems. The General Ledger may be integrated with various scheduling and project management tools to leverage optimisation and automation.

As there are many types of accounting and project management software tools, system integration and automation can become complex and expensive. This framework recommends that system integration and automation should be staged – get your foundations right before adding the bolt-ons. Over time this integration and automation will yield significant benefits, both financial and non-financial.

6.1 Organisational rules, policies and/or procedures

The least expensive, and arguably least effective method of ensuring financial tracking consistency between accounting and project management tools are organisational rules, policies and/or procedures. The importance of having rules, policies and procedures in place should not be underestimated, however, if these are not followed or engrained into the ways-of-working of an organisation, these will not be effective. As staff turnover occurs, continuous refreshers of the ways-of-working are required.

These rules, policies and procedures must dictate how the accounting and project management reporting is to happen if there is no system automation and integration.

Rules, policies and/or procedures must at a minimum include (documented or not):
- Responsibilities of the Project team in providing timely information to the Accounting Division (potentially through using a Project Accountant).
- Responsibilities of the (Project) Accountant in providing timely information to the Project team and Project Board/Sponsor and/or Executive Board.
- How this information is to be tracked and presented to various interested and responsible parties, as well as frequency.
- The review process of the information required to be presented.
- Defined terms of reference, as each team and organisation may have a different meaning for similar sounding terms and acronyms (as mentioned previously there is no consistency in the industry for the meaning of OPEX and benefits. The same can be said for CAPEX).
- Escalation points and dispute resolution.
- Delegations of authority for approvals of spend (contracts and payments).

In practice: We have seen numerous ways Project teams and Accountants work together on reporting results. These range from MS PowerPoint presentations, where the Project Accountants are responsible for the financial slides, to data input into project management tools to report projects and portfolios thereof in a more virtual environment. How this reporting is done is manual and hence, requires documentation to ensure that consistency is maintained. Unfortunately, manual data entry means that it is also prone to error and data manipulation.

6.2 System integration and automation

To truly ensure financial tracking consistency, this framework recommends system integration and automation of various project accounting activities. Below are considerations for the type of activities that can be automated and integrated:

1. *Time sheeting integrated with the General Ledger* – this is generally one of the first integrations that organisations embark upon, as it is inefficient to manually populate timesheet data into a separate system to keep track of labour costs.

2. *Procurement automation and integration with Accounts Payable and Accounts Receivable functions.* If this works seamlessly (which in practice is rare), there are significant productivity, data integrity and transparency benefits. If it is possible to add delegations of authority approvals process or a contracts management tool for this integration, then there are additional productivity benefits.

3. *Automate financial project tracking* – this means having an inbuilt system functionality where projects are tracked from a financial perspective. This can be a module that plugs into existing project or accounting software where all financial metrics and project finances are tracked.

4. *Time sheeting integrated with Scheduling tools* – if scheduling tools are used by a project or there are other project management tools used to track effort and task completion. This is a handy integration to understand the completion of Sprints or Milestones and the velocity being used rather than the Scrum Master or Project Manager required to do manual calculations.

5. *Capitalisation and metric calculations* – this functionality can be inbuilt into various financial systems that are tracking projects. This is considered a nice to have but can save your Accountants time in doing the calculations manually every time.

6.3 Other points of consideration

6.3.1 Regulatory and taxation requirements

When embarking on any form of automation, consideration is required for regulation and taxation requirements. This may be regulation and guidelines related to Accounting and other industry standards, where certain benchmarks are required to be upheld as a minimum. These types of requirements may relate to segregation of duties, system controls, security measures, etc. Hence, varied consultation of potential stakeholders is required before embarking on system automation and/or integration.

As regulation changes over time, making sure that the systems in place are updated is vital. If this is not done, organisations may detriment themselves in a variety of ways including fines, incorrect taxation treatments, breaches of contracts, etc. Organisations spend significant amounts of money ensuring their systems are up to date.

6.3.2 Assets register

This is a separate register outside the General Ledger to keep a record of all assets, whether physical or virtual, owned or created by the organisation. This register track assets across the organisation and helps calculate depreciation and amortisation for each asset. This type of register is manually upheld by either the Procurement and/or Accounting team(s). Integration of such a register with a General Ledger is possible, bearing in mind that the bigger the organisation, the more complex the task of ensuring the Assets register is maintained correctly.

6.3.3 OPEX and Benefits tracking

This is one of the most complex integrations or automations an organisation can attempt. This framework recommends that an organisation attempts to embark on this activity only once all other project accounting activities discussed above have been automated/integrated. Systems need to talk to each other seamlessly in order to attempt automating or integrating OPEX and benefits for a project. In practice, the closest organisations come to automation or integration of this activity is ensuring there is some form of manual functionality inbuilt into existing project tracking software.

The reason this is so complex has been implied in previous Steps and will be discussed further in **Step 7: Benefits and OPEX** – projects impact various aspects of the business at the same time and multiple projects can impact the same business area simultaneously. Attributing benefits to specific projects can be very complex, especially as time progresses and the validity of benefits is questioned.

KEY TAKEAWAYS

- System integration and automation should be staged.

- To ensure financial tracking consistency between accounting and project management tools, set up rules, policies and/or procedures across the organisation and maintain relevancy.

- Mitigate risk by ensuring you consider up-to-date regulatory and taxation requirements.

Step 7: Benefits and OPEX

The main reason for organisations to invest in projects is for eventual return on their investment (ROI). Another way of looking at this is organisations spend money in order to make money. This type of investment is assessed on the variety of benefits it will generate i.e. cost reductions, revenue increases, etc. Apart from generating benefits, projects also have ongoing upkeep costs, referred to as ongoing operating expenses (OPEX) that pay for ongoing support of the changes that a project generates.

This framework has briefly introduced the concepts of benefits and OPEX in section *2.5 Future Project Implications: Introduction to Benefits and Ongoing Operational Expenses (OPEX).* As previously noted, there is no standardisation in terminology used across the industry, nor are there clear guidelines as to how benefits and OPEX should be managed within project delivery approaches. For simplicity purposes, this framework defines benefits and OPEX as follows:

- *Benefits* are positive impacts to a division or organisation as a whole derived from a project deliverable. Benefits are tangible (hard) or intangible (soft), as well as, quantitative or qualitative. Benefits can be negative, provided these are either qualitative or relate to a negative impact on revenue generation.
  Simply put, think of benefits as an impact on Revenue.

- Ongoing *operating expenses (OPEX)* are negative quantitative impacts to a division or organisation as a whole derived from a project deliverable. This is a cost that is specifically related to an increase or decrease in expenses.
  Simply put, think of OPEX as an impact on Expenses.

As previously noted, *first-year OPEX* usually has a negative project implication derived from the project during its delivery timeframe and must be included in the business case for the project. The reason behind the project including this first-year cost is primarily due to budgetary practicality and secondly to ensure all projects costs are appropriately captured.

Benefits and OPEX are a major part of determining the success or failure of a project, however, these can be challenging to track. Project delivery approach does not delve into details as to how benefits and OPEX are to be managed or tracked as the Project Manager or Product Owner transfers this responsibility to another party once the project itself is deemed complete. This framework recommends that clear lines of responsibility are agreed upon. A tracking mechanism for benefits and OPEX is required to be established prior to the project being deemed complete. Whether this is done during various retrospectives or at the closure phase of the project does not make a difference, it just needs to be done.

Tracking the benefits and OPEX derived from the project(s) is as important as tracking the cost of the same project, yet, it is significantly more challenging to do so. Hence, many organisations do not embark on this exercise at all or to a very limited extent. The use of rough estimates and assumption-driven forecasts is not an appropriate way to track the benefits and OPEX of projects. However, due to continuous restructures and the dynamic nature of most organisations, tracking benefits and OPEX through divisions ends up an ever-difficult task. In these cases, organisations and Executive Boards need to be honest with themselves and in many cases, may either need to establish very clear tracking mechanisms or abandon certain benefit tracking exercises as futile attempts at tracking the untraceable.

7.1 Tangible and Intangible Benefits

Benefits are tangible or intangible (sometimes referred to as hard or soft, respectively):
- *Tangible benefits* are quantitative and measurable. These are benefits that have a clear monetary value attributable to them. These benefits are attributed to but are not exclusively related to reductions in labour/expenses, increases in revenue and other trackable benefits.

- *Intangible benefits* are qualitative, harder to measure and can be subjective or perception based. These benefits may have a value attributable to them, which in reality is rarely trackable through the organisation's financial accounts, as these are indirectly linked. These benefits predominantly relate to soft targets, such as productivity increases, cost avoidance, increased satisfaction, etc, all of which are important benefits.

As tangible benefits are predominantly trackable in order to ensure that ROI has been achieved, mature organisations implement a mechanism by which budgets will reflect the promised benefits or increased OPEX. An example of this can be observed in *Example 2.5.*

Example 2.5:
Project X had committed to deliver $100k p.a. in revenue increases and $10k p.a. in productivity savings by introducing a new product.

The Sales and Product Division has agreed that this project will deliver the revenue increase which will be recognised in the accounts of this division. The IT Division has agreed that the project will deliver the productivity savings, however, noted that these will be challenging to track and are estimates only.

How should the budget, post project completion, be reflecting the above benefits?
- The Sales and Product Division's budget for the following year will reflect an incremental increase in revenue targets by $100 p.a.
- The IT Division's budget should NOT reflect the incremental productivity savings of $10k p.a. unless there is a clear trackable mechanism for this saving. This type of mechanism is to be established when compiling a business case or lean canvas and is to drive the optimal impact for the organisation.

Note: Any benefits that have been built into the budget must be reassessed on a semi-annual/annual basis to ensure these are still valid and any project capitalisation is not impaired.

7.2 Tracking Benefits and OPEX

Tangible benefits should be tracked by the *project sponsor*. A *project sponsor* could be an individual, a division or multiples thereof that have signed up to those benefits being achieved. By signing up to a benefit, as noted in **Example 2.5,** the project sponsor expects that the project achieves the ROI it has set out to achieve and that the benefits and OPEX delivered will then impact the future financial accounts of the organisation. The project sponsor may delegate the task of tracking benefits and OPEX to the Project Accountant, PMO and/or Project Manager while the project is still in delivery.

Tracking of benefits and OPEX is required until a *run rate* is achieved. A *run rate* is the quantitative amount that is achieved through a consistent realisation of the same result every month. Using **Example 2.5,** this would be the $100k p.a. achieved through the consistent monthly income of $8,300 per month (i.e. $100k/12 months). Realistically, income could vary from month-to-month, hence, it may be more appropriate to look at the yearly amount of income attributed to the project benefit. The same case is for OPEX, only in reverse.

Once a run rate is achieved, monthly tracking can be stopped and instead occasional reassessment of benefits should occur on a half-yearly basis (this is also a requirement for any impairment of assets created by the project). This should be done until either of the two occurs first:
- ROI is achieved; or
- All assets created by the project are fully depreciated/amortised.

Depending on the size of the project and organisation, the project accountant could be involved with tracking the benefits and OPEX while the project is in delivery phase. Once the project is deemed complete, the benefits and OPEX profile is handed over to the business-as-usual (BAU) finance team (aka Finance/Accounting Division) and is embedded as part of the ongoing budgets of the organisation. These requirements are driven by Accounting Standards that dictate impairment testing and asset value. Please refer to **3.2 Asset creation: Depreciation, Amortisation and Impairment Testing** for an in-depth explanation.

There is no single way of tracking benefits and OPEX that t this framework can prescribe. Instead, this framework recommends that regardless of how the tracking occurs, be mindful of some common pitfalls that organisations have experienced that have led to gross under/over-statement of benefits and/or OPEX (this is not a finite list):

- *Double counting of benefits across multiple projects*
  This happens often when there is no common register of benefits and OPEX in an organisation. This is particularly common when external consultants are brought in to analyse benefits for a project as the approach is siloed and there is no exploration done into other projects and the benefits claimed by them.

- *Contract mismanagement*
  Organisations often have many parties managing relationships and contracts with vendors involved in delivering projects. Unfortunately, this creates a lack of centralisation and hence, a lack of understanding as to where each contract stands in relation to each other. This is common where the same vendor is involved in multiple projects and may have negotiated higher or lower benefits or OPEX with the hiring organisation.

- *Staff reduction vs reallocation*
  This is a common misconception for many projects – what is the point at which a reduction in staff is a monetary benefit to the project? Is it if the staff leave the organisation altogether or if they fill roles in other teams? Unless the staff have physically left the organisation, there is no ongoing expense reduction for the organisation. This may be common sense but is forgotten while business cases and lean canvases are compiled. The other point of consideration is redundancy, retrenchment and retraining costs. These can be expensive and the project should pay for these costs unless there is a different agreement with the project sponsor.

- *Accounting for benefits, but forgetting OPEX*
  Project Managers and Product Owners are often focused on painting the most positive picture of their ideas to the Project Boards/Sponsors

and Executive Boards. Commonly, but rarely intentionally, OPEX is often forgotten or under-budgeted for the project.

- *Claiming unrealistic benefits, which are then eroded*
This pitfall goes back to the discussion of tangible versus intangible benefits. Intangible benefits although important, are dangerous to sign-up to due to their lack of trackability. This does not stop the excitement of the project business case and lean canvas to include these in the ROI. When these are included in the ROI they bring unrealistic expectations for the project performance and can then impact the Project Manager's and Project Team's KPIs. This framework recommends that if quantitative intangible benefits are included in ROI, then two separate ROIs and NPVs should be presented (the latter excluding the intangible benefits).

Note: This framework stresses that there is nothing wrong with pursuing a project with a negative NPV or a less than desirable ROI i.e. there may be regulatory or compliance required projects. In fact, many projects are pursued for strategic reasons, where the intangible benefits are significant, however, untraceable. In these cases, the project stakeholders are being honest with themselves and the organisation and do not agree with signing up to budget reductions or increases on the basis of intangible benefits.

- *Contractual price sensitivity and inflation*
Many projects need to be aware that by the time their projects are completed there may be an erosion of the benefits claimed. This can be due to the way vendor contracts and other external factors impact industry and the business environment. Many contracts have in-built clauses for the type of ongoing services and attributable OPEX that the organisation will likely pay, as well as inbuilt inflationary measures. Some contracts have minimal spends and if the organisation decides to suddenly downsize and upscale, there can be significant repercussions to contracts. In building and then tracking benefits and OPEX, all contractual obligations need to be built into the business case.

- *Re-baselining benefits and OPEX*
  Some industries and price points move significantly due to innovation, disruption, seasonality, etc. This may mean that using current costs as baselines to compare with future costs in order to calculate the uplift in benefits or OPEX may become quickly redundant. By the time long-term projects are completed (especially transformation projects) the original baseline being used to compare with is redundant. Reassessment of the original baseline may be required due to the number of external aspects that may impact the project.

- *Project impact can be difficult to attribute to a single project*
  This is the most challenging pitfall, as most projects organisations embark upon, are small. These projects make incremental changes to the way that business is done and most of these are difficult to track. In order to track changes, specifically related to financial implications brought about by a project, the change may need to be significant enough to be noticeable. This is why benefits are often tracked using assumptions. This framework recommends investing in analytical tools to help project impact be tracked appropriately.

7.3 Lean Accounting & Agile Delivery Approach: Benefits & OPEX Tracking

Lean accounting and agile delivery approach accommodate for a much more fluid environment for projects. Rather than working in yearly budgeting cycles and longer-term project benefit realisation cycles, lean accounting looks at ROI and KPI delivery on a quarterly basis (Parmenter, 2016). This means that KPIs are set on a quarterly basis for an organisation to achieve and the projects and BAU activities run during this time are accountable to show what has been achieved during this timeframe.

In practice, this type of working environment accommodates the agile delivery approach delivery in a much better way. As agile delivery approach looks at faster delivery and risk reduction in a shorter timeframe for a project, it should deliver benefits faster as well. Please see *Example 2.6* for an overview.

Example 2.6: Agile project tracking in a lean accounting environment:

$'k	Jul-01	Aug-01	Sep-01	Q1	...	Total FY01
BAU Revenue Forecast	200	200	200	600	...	2,400
BAU Cost Forecast	(100)	(100)	(100)	(300)	...	(1,200)
BAU P&L Forecast	**100**	**100**	**100**	**300**	...	**1,200**
Project Cost Forecast	(500)	(500)	-	(1,000)	-	(1,000)
Project Incremental Benefits Forecast	*50*	*50*	*50*	*150*	...	*600*
Total Project F'cast	**(450)**	**(450)**	**50**	**(850)**	...	**(400)**
Total P&L Forecast	***(350)***	***(350)***	***150***	***(550)***	...	***(800)***

Instead of the above Total FY01 being the budget set for the year, it becomes an "indicative budget" only with the quarterly forecast e.g. Q1 becoming the more important metric to measure against from a KPI perspective. This would mean that the above project forecast can be broken into the following fortnightly Sprints:

$'k	Sprint 1	Sprint 2	Sprint 3	Sprint 4	Sprint 5	Sprint 6	Q1
Project Cost Forecast	(100)	(400)	(300)	(200)	-	-	(1,000)
Project Opex Forecast	(100)	(150)	(200)	(200)	(200)	(200)	(1,050)
Project Benefits F'cast	110	190	225	225	225	225	1,200
Project Incremental Benefits Forecast	*10*	*40*	*25*	*25*	*25*	*25*	*150*
Total Project F'cast	**(90)**	**(360)**	**(275)**	**(175)**	**25**	**25**	**(850)**

The above is setting out the KPIs against which a project will be measured on a monthly basis to meet the required Q1 forecast, rather than yearly budget.

7.4 Modelling Benefits and OPEX

There is no prescribed way of modelling benefits and OPEX – it all depends on the organisation's way of working and accountability requirements.

One way of thinking about modelling benefits and OPEX is all about the drivers corresponding to these benefits and OPEX. Driver benefits modelling looks at triggers to help determine the point at which realisation of benefits and OPEX occurs. This will not necessarily help track the actual financial benefit or OPEX, but this approach will help determine whether the triggers for the benefits have occurred and hence, benefits are realised.

Another way of thinking about modelling benefits and OPEX is concentrating only on those benefits and OPEX that can be traced through financial accounts. This may involve fairly complex analytics that can be set up in the background of various systems in order to determine how much of a specific expense or income has been attributable to various projects. The question here is whether this activity is in fact value-add and to what extent it is important to the organisation investing its resources. *Example 2.7* below looks at types of benefits and OPEX and how these can be triggered and tracked:

Example 2.7:
You are looking at buying your own house, which will be significantly bigger than the current rental property that you occupy. This house will cost you $1m to buy and will bring you a number of benefits and ongoing costs (OPEX):
1. $25k p.a. – you will no longer pay rent on your current rental property.
2. $50k p.a. – interest on your mortgage that has been borrowed to build the house.
3. $10k p.a. – you will no longer pay utility bills on your current rental property.
4. $20k p.a. – in utility bills for the new house.
5. $5k p.a. – less cleaning and maintaining (corresponds to hours of your time).

Example 2.7 (continued):

6. $20k p.a. – cleaning & maintaining a bigger place (increase in hours of your time).
7. Sense of satisfaction from buying your own home.
8. Ability to make adjustments to your own home as opposed to a rental that had restrictions.
9. Enjoyment of more space than the rental property.
10. Anxiety from the $1m debt that is required to be repaid.

These ten benefits / OPEX correspond to the below:

No.	Benefit/ OPEX	Tangible/ Intangible	Driver	$'k p.a.
1	Benefit	Tangible	Cancellation of rental agreement.	25
2	OPEX	N/A	Signing of mortgage contract with bank.	(50)
3	Benefit	Tangible	Cancellation of utility contracts for rental property.	10
4	OPEX	N/A	Signing of new utility contracts for new house.	(20)
5	Benefit	Tangible	Stop cleaning and maintaining the rental property.	5
6	OPEX	N/A	Start cleaning and maintaining the new house.	(20)
7	Benefit	Intangible	Walking into the new house.	-
8	Benefit	Intangible	The first time you hang a painting in your house.	-
9	Benefit	Intangible	Purchase of new furniture for a bigger place.	-
10	Benefit	Intangible	Signing the mortgage contract with the bank. **Note:** this is a negative intangible benefit.	-
			Total net benefits/(OPEX) p.a.	**(50)**

In other words, this $1m investment is going to additionally cost you $50k per annum, which means both a negative ROI and NPV. This is where the investor must question whether it is worth buying this house.

Now that there is clarity around the drivers, the tracking of these benefits and OPEX is important.

Example 2.7 (continued):

Here is how this framework recommends tracking said benefits and OPEX.

No.	Tracking mechanism	Evidence	Potential pitfalls
1	Once rental agreement is cancelled, ensure payment of rent is terminated.	Bank statement	Direct debits not cancelled.
2	Once the first payment of the mortgage is made ensure calculations are set up to predict future payments for forecasting.	Bank statement	Undisclosed fees and charges.
3	Once utility contracts are cancelled, ensure payment of bills is terminated.	Bank statement	Direct debits not cancelled.
4	Contracts for new utility bills can be used to predict future payments (ensure to adjust for seasonality).	Bills	Contracts having variable rates.
5	Track hours used to spend on cleaning and maintaining of rental property (use this as a baseline).	Tracking app	Insufficient tracking leads to incorrect baseline.
6	Track hours required to clean and maintain the new house.	Tracking app	This can be significantly less or more than the expected original amount of $20k hours equivalent p.a.
7 - 10	This framework recommends not spending time on tracking these intangible benefits. These may be significant intangible benefits and the main reasons for investing in a house, however, tracking these will not be a value-add activity overall to the project.		

There are various software applications that can track the tangible benefits and OPEX. The most common of these is Microsoft Excel. However, if it is possible to capture these in an existing ledger this will ensure that ROI is captured in the one place and data therefore becomes more manageable.

7.5 Balance Sheet and Profit & Loss Impact of Benefits and OPEX

Similar to Project cost, benefits and OPEX impact both Balance Sheet, mostly in form of cash and accruals; and Profit and Loss, depending on whether the impact is on revenue or expenses. The concept of *first-year OPEX* has been discussed in *2.5 Future Project Implications: Introduction to Benefits and Ongoing Operational Expenses (OPEX).* This section concentrates on the practicality of the impact of benefits and OPEX as part of project projections for the organisation after the project finalisation.

Example 2.8: Project X is estimated to cost $100k over the next 4 months. The following assumptions have been made:

- The Project will span over 2 financial years i.e. Yr 1 & Yr 2 (assume $25k per month in spend).
- The $100k spend is made up of $90k software development spend (i.e. capitalisable) and $10k travel spend (i.e. expensed).
- The $10k travel cost will be spent wholly in the first month.
- Amortisation of the software will start once the project is deemed to go-live.
- After the first month's deliverable, the project will deliver $10k p.a. (paid up-front) in OPEX and $20k (paid up front) in benefits.
- When the project is complete, the tangible benefits will increase to $75k p.a.

Category ($'k)	Yr 1	Yr 2	Yr 3	Yr 4	Yr 5	Total
Project Cash Cost	(50)	(50)				(100)
1st Year OPEX	(10)					(10)
Total Project Cash Cost* (A)	**(60)**	**(50)**				**(110)**
Travel & 1st Year OPEX	(20)					(20)
SW Dev Amortisation (3yrs)	-	(25)	(30)	(30)	(5)	(90)
Total Project P&L Cost* (B)	**(20)**	**(25)**	**(30)**	**(30)**	**(5)**	**(110)**
Ongoing OPEX (C)	-	(10)	(10)	(10)	(10)	(40)
Benefits (D)	20	75	75	75	75	320
Total Cash Impact (A+C+D)	**(40)**	**15**	**65**	**65**	**65**	**170**
Total P&L Impact (B+C+D)	**-**	**40**	**35**	**35**	**60**	**170**

*Notice that the Total Project Cash Cost and Total Project P&L Cost equate to the same value over time.

Example 2.8 (continued):

Taking this example one step further, the benefits and OPEX delivered for the software development project are assumed to be as follows:

1. The $10k p.a. in OPEX is for a licence cost to an external vendor for the maintenance and upkeep of the software.
*   The initial $20k p.a. in benefits, which increases to $75k p.a. is:
    2. an increase in revenue of $50k p.a. from a new upgrade to an existing product for the Sales team;
    3. a reduction in manual IT staff work of $25k p.a. (assuming this staff member works part-time and leaves the organisation).

The above benefits and OPEX could be recognised as follows, assuming the organisation is structured into divisions proposed by this example:

Profit/Loss	Division	Impact $'k	Balance Sheet	Division	Impact $'k
1. Revenue	Sales	↑ 50	1. Cash	Sales	↑ 50
2. Expenses	IT	↑ (10)	2. Cash	IT	↑ (10)
3. Expenses	IT	↓ 25	3. Cash	IT	↓ 25
Amortisation	Finance	↑ (30)			
Total P&L Impact**		**35**	**Total Cash Impact****		**65**

**This is the annualised impact of the project on the organisation. Note this impact occurs in Yr 3 post the project delivery.

Example 2.8 examines the impact of project benefits and OPEX on the organisation as the project delivers these future implications.

7.6 Project Metrics vs BAU Budgets

When a project business case or lean canvas is compiled, there are various metrics used to calculate whether a project should be funded. Please refer to **2.7 Project Metrics** for the more commonly used project metrics. A reassessment of whether the project should be continued is at times done at various stages of the project lifecycle. Unfortunately, there is one major pitfall at play when reassessments are done post the first financial year of the project (if the project lasts through multiple financial years). This is related to BAU budgets.

BAU budgets account for benefit and OPEX profiles that a project is to deliver. As alluded to previously in this step, when a project is approved to be funded by an internal or external client to whom the benefits or OPEX belong (post the *first-year OPEX*) these benefits or OPEX become part of their budgets in future years. This pitfall is represented in **Example 2.9.**

Example 2.9:

Referring to *Example 2.8,* below is an initial project financial plan. Assuming the project was given funding, the first 3 years will suffice to demonstrate the required changes:

Category ($'k)	Yr 1	Yr 2	Yr 3	...	Total
Project Cash Cost	(50)	(50)			(100)
1st Year OPEX	(10)				(10)
Total Project Cash Cost (A)	**(60)**	**(50)**			**(110)**
Travel & 1st Year OPEX	(20)			...	(20)
SW Dev Amortisation (3yrs)	-	(25)	(30)	-	(55)
Total Project P&L Cost* (B)	**(20)**	**(25)**	**(30)**	**...**	**(75)**
Ongoing OPEX (C)	-	(10)	(10)	...	(20)
Benefits (D)	20	75	75	...	170
Total Cash Impact (A+C+D)	**(40)**	**15**	**65**	**...**	**40**
Total P&L Impact (B+C+D)	**-**	**40**	**35**	**-**	**75**

The above would have been loaded into the client's budget for the next 3 years and the Yr 1 project budget would have been equivalent to the BAU budget.

Assume that the initial BAU budget is $500k p.a. and that:
- OPEX is a $10k p.a. increase in licensing costs, but this increase only happens once, i.e. the cost base from a BAU perspective increases and will remain at this increased rate for the next 5 years.
- The initial $20k p.a. in benefits, which increases to $75k p.a. is a reduction in staff costs of $25k p.a. and increase in revenue of $50k p.a., but again these changes only happen once i.e. the client will lower their staff costs by $25k once, when the part-time staff member leaves and revenue will increase to the additional amount of $50k p.a. and stay at that increased amount.

As the project would have finished by the time this profile is delivered, the BAU budget is where these incremental changes are required and hence the budget for Yr 2 onwards will only require the incremental amendment.

For Yr 3 there are no changes.

Example 2.9 (continued):

From a BAU budgetary perspective only incremental changes should ever be made.

Incorrect reflection of the business case in BAU budget:

Budget ($'k)	Yr 1	Yr 2	Yr 3
Baseline BAU Budget	500	520	585
OPEX	-	(10)	(10)
Benefits	20	75	75
New BAU Budget	**520**	**585**	**650**

The pitfall occurs due to the incorrect understanding of the data in the project business case.

Correct reflection of the business case in BAU budget:

Budget ($'k)	Yr 1	Yr 2	Yr 3
Baseline BAU Budget	500	520	565
Incremental OPEX	-	(10)	-
Incremental Benefits	20	55	-
New BAU Budget	**520**	**565**	**565**

Unless the project is incrementally increasing its benefits and OPEX every year i.e. reducing the same amount of staff annually and increasing the payment for licensing due to a contractual obligation, the budget will quickly become over-inflated.

Hence, being aware of the purpose of project metrics versus how project benefits and OPEX are accounted for in budgets is very important.

KEY TAKEAWAYS

- Benefits are positive impacts derived from a project deliverable.

- Tangible benefits are quantitative and measurable.

- Intangible benefits are qualitative, harder to measure and can be subjective and perception based.

- Benefits can be negative, provided these are qualitative or relate to a decrease in revenue.

- Ongoing operating expenses (OPEX) are negative quantitative impacts derived from a project deliverable.

- First-year OPEX is a negative project implication derived from the project during its delivery timeframe.

- There is no prescribed way of modelling benefits and OPEX – it all depends on the organisation's way of working and accountability requirements.

- Companies with lean accounting create a better environment for projects using agile delivery approach to succeed in.

- Make sure that only incremental changes delivered by a project are made in BAU budgets.

Step 8: Reporting

Financial reports provide insights and help drive decision making for projects by Sponsors and Executive Boards. These reports need to be simple and straight to the point. A common barrier for accountants has been related to the convoluted way that financial information is presented. This process of reporting should use layman's terms and data visualisation techniques to drive a required outcome.

This framework recommends that the Project Accountant or a representative of the Accounting division is present when financial decisions are being made for project(s). So that those decisions are then clearly represented in future financial reports and are reported accurately to other stakeholders.

Please see **Example 3.0** of a monthly dashboard that should be provided to Steering Committees, Executive Boards and/or Sponsors to facilitate decision making.

Example 3.0:
Project dashboard for the month of May-01, reported in Jun-01 using **Example 2.1** and extra assumptions below:

- The hardware is depreciated over 5 years and one fifth will be included this year;
- 1st year OPEX is $5k. It is expensed and benefits are expected to be $20k and are tracked as part of the project but included in the Sponsor's budget rather than the project's (see **Step 7: Benefits and OPEX** for the explanation);
- Apart from depreciation and 1st year OPEX, the project is expecting to spend $20k in P&L budget in 2001.

Example 3.0 (continued):

$'k (rounded)	Monthly Variance			YTD Variance			FY01 Project Variance				E2E Project Variance			
	Actual	F'cast	Var %	Actual	F'cast	Var %	EAC	Budget	Var $	Var %	EAC	Budget	Var $	Var %
Resources	26	33	21%	26	33	21%	76	78	2	2%	76	78	2	2%
Non-Resources	-	10	100%	-	10	100%	10	10	-	-	10	10	-	-
Total	26	43	17%	26	43	17%	86	88	2	2%	86	88	2	2%
Depreciation	-	2	100%	-	2	100%	-	2	2	100%	10	10	-	-
1ˢᵗ yr OPEX	-	-	-	-	-	-	5	5	-	-	5	5	-	-
Total Project P&L	-	2	100%	-	2	100%	25	27	2	7%	27	27	-	-
Total Project Cash	26	43	17%	-	43	17%	93	95	2	2%	93	95	2	2%
Benefits	-	-	-	-	-	-	20	20	-	-	200	200	-	-
OPEX	-	-	-	-	-	-	-	-	-	-	50	50	-	-

Var % = (Forecast – Actual) / Forecast x 100 OR Var % = Var $ / Budget x 100

Insights:

1. Permanent variance: immaterial resources underspend of $2k (2%) (refer to **Example 2.1** as to how this was calculated) for End-to-End Project.

2. Timing variance: resources underspend of $5k and non-resource underspend of $10k (refer to **Example 2.1**).

3. The $10k non-resource timing variance is related to the purchase of hardware, whose depreciation lifecycle is pushed into FY02, reducing P&L variance for FY01 by $2k (7%).

Note: from a data visualisation perspective, positive or negative variance percentages are highlighting how good the Project team is at forecasting for their coming Sprint or monthly spend. +/- 5% is Light Grey, +/- 6-10% is Medium Grey, > 10% is Dark Grey meaning the higher the percentage the worse the forecasting.

8.1 Reflecting decisions in financials

Many project stakeholders do not realise that project decisions impact financial reporting statements. Project Accountants refresh this information to ensure no surprises occur toward financial deadlines and to ensure management is aware if there is insufficient or too much funding available for project investment.

A graphical technique allows project stakeholders to see how the project is tracking in a quick visual snapshot. This linear graph representation (as shown in *Example 3.1*) compares the cumulative approved project investment budget to the latest estimate at completion (EAC). On the same graph, it is often useful to see the monthly spend compared with that month's forecast to give an indication to the project stakeholders how each month is tracking.

Example 3.1:
Using *Example 2.1 & 3.0* the following would be a graphic representation as at the end of May-01 for the project.

Project as at May-01

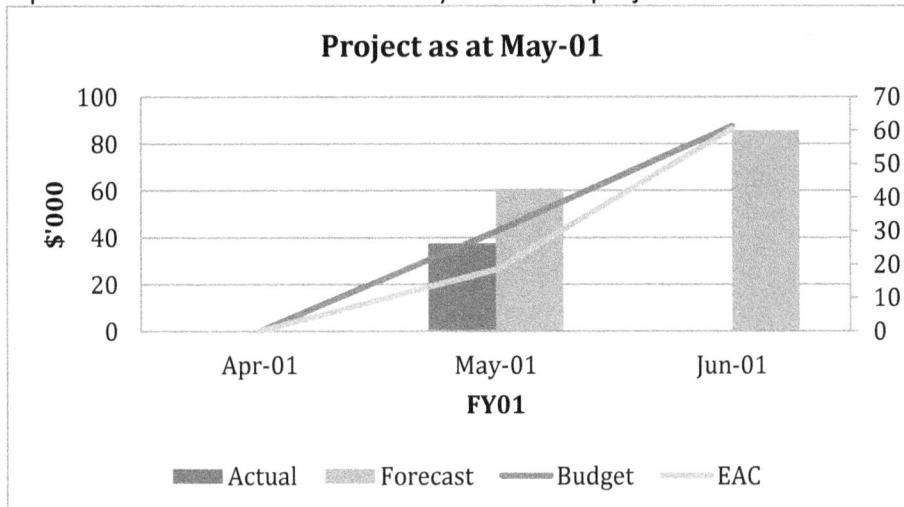

This form of graphical representation is also done for the entire portfolio of projects to best capture a snapshot of where the overall portfolio investment is at a point in time and how it impacts organisational strategy. Please see **Step 9: Portfolio and Prioritisation** for further information.

The Accounting Division must also reflect the capitalisation decisions that are made for projects, as well as, the benefits and OPEX that are to come into BAU in the various financial reports to the company's stakeholders. As previously mentioned, these decisions must be reassessed on a half-yearly and yearly basis to ensure that the decisions made in the past are still valid. For example, an asset that was created a year ago for a company is no longer used to the extent expected and is not yielding the benefits promised and hence, may require a revaluation or impairment on the Balance Sheet.

Note: A common metric used by the Accounting Division to estimate projects is the run-rate of the project to compare how projects are tracking to the budget allocated. If the project is a long-term project, this metric can be helpful as to give a quick and basic answer to expected project monthly spend. But beware, where project spend is highly volatile, or the project is a fast deliverable i.e. 3 months, this metric can grossly over/under-estimate the project.

8.2 Reporting to decision makers

Apart from information being concise and visually represented, reporting to decision makers must also be timely and in a format, that ensures the attention of the decision maker. Information that is late in the month or in email format, where the decision maker is time-poor and rarely gets through their inbox, is redundant.

8.3 Integration of financial reporting

As discussed in **Step 6: Systems,** one way to ensure financial reporting occurs seamlessly and accurately is to create automated reports that generate the required financial information monthly, with the Project Accountant providing insights into the information using dashboard or project management reporting tools. Provided it is in a similar format as the rest of the project information provided on a monthly/Sprint basis, this can be very timely and helpful to all project stakeholders, as well as, drive project transparency.

KEY TAKEAWAYS

- Project financial reports should use data visualisation techniques and avoid jargon to present the project status.

- Decisions made for projects should be reflected in the organisation's financials.

- Teams and/or organisations can use a visual graph to give a graphical snapshot of the project comparing cumulative budget and project estimate at completion.

- Run-rate to forecast projects should be avoided as this type of analysis can grossly under/over-estimate spend.

Step 9: Portfolio and prioritisation

So far, **Steps 1-8** of this framework discussed in depth project accounting for individual projects. However, many organisations do not run individual projects one at a time; instead many projects are run simultaneously. This is where portfolio management and prioritisation becomes important. Especially as organisations often have a finite amount of project investment that they can spend in the one year (see **Step 3: Impact: CAPEX and Value**). Hence, the projects that have the potential to yield the best returns or strategic outcomes should be given priority.

Budgets are often set for several years in advance i.e. many company stakeholders demand 3-5-year budgets in many industries. To accommodate this, accountants look at project prioritisation a lot further in advance than projects have even been conceptualised. This means that projects are expected to commit to bringing in benefits for many years to come by agreeing to projects that have not as yet been conceptualised. Hence, when ideas for projects come up to achieve those benefits, priorities change depending on the benefits profile. This activity is referred to as portfolio management and prioritisation.

"Who screams the loudest": Approach to prioritisation

In practice, project portfolio prioritisation can be an enormously challenging exercise, with some organisations often running hundreds of projects simultaneously. Experience shows that large organisations often prioritise projects based on either Project Sponsor relationships with the Executive Board or by using the premise of "who screams the loudest". Note, this can be an incredible waste of effort and monetary spend, with little benefit to the organisation.

9.1 What do we Start, Stop, Continue? : Portfolio decision making

When organisations run multiple projects simultaneously, the question of how to prioritise the existing ideas and potential projects can be challenging to answer. Here, it is often helpful to look at the decision-making process through the lens of "Start, Stop, Continue". This process is used in the following way for projects:

START	STOP	CONTINUE
Projects that have higher NPVs/ROIs than the current portfolio of projects or expected WACC. Projects that have low MVP costs, but have potential strategic benefits or high earned value.	Projects whose benefits profile has been eroded. Projects that are not aligned with the organisation's strategy or expected earned value.	Projects that have an NPV/ROI that is consistent with expectations. Projects that are strategically aligned with the organisation and are expected to bring in expected value.

The metrics assessments discussed in *2.7 Project metrics* and earned value analysis (EVA) discussed in *5.4 Earned value analysis and KPI output* can help Executive Boards, Project Boards and/or Sponsors decide whether a project should be prioritised and what its priority should be as compared with other projects. There is an additional metric that (Brown, et al., 2016) describes as helpful in deciding between projects. This metric is known as the Equivalent annual cash flow (equivalent annual annuity) and it looks at comparing projects' financial returns with different project lifecycles and risk profiles. Please note that some projects may not have expected cash flows and this metric will not be helpful in making decisions whether to invest in such projects. This framework recommends using other metrics targeted at start-up companies in this case.

- Equivalent annual annuity (EAA) is a technique that converts a project's NPV into a uniform series of cash flows, enabling the comparison of projects with different project lifecycles and risk profiles, based on the annual value that they add (or based on being repeatable in perpetuity). The project with the higher EAA should be chosen (Brown, et al., 2016).

$$EAA_{t=n} = \frac{NPV_{t=n}}{Annuity\ factor}$$

$$Annuity\ factor_{t=n} = \frac{1 - (1 + i)^{-n}}{i}$$

Where:
NPV = net present value of a project
Annuity factor = present value of $1 received annually for n years of project lifecycle
i = average discount rate during the lifecycle period
n = number of periods or project lifecycle

Example 3.2: The organisation is deciding whether to invest in Project X or Project Y. The discount rate for both projects is 10%.

$'000	Project X	Project Y
Initial investment	(100)	(100)
Net cash flows		
Yr 1	75	50
Yr 2	75	50
Yr 3		50
NPV (rounded)	30	24

Annuity factors:

$$Annuity\ factor\ (Project\ X)_{t=2} = \frac{1-(1+0.1)^{-2}}{0.1} = 1.7355$$

$$Annuity\ factor\ (Project\ Y)_{t=3} = \frac{1-(1\pm0.1)^{-3}}{0.1} = 2.4869$$

The following EAAs will indicate which project to invest in:

$$EAA\ (Project\ X)_{t=2} = \frac{30}{1.7355} = 17.286\ or\ \$17,286$$

$$EAA\ (Project\ Y)_{t=3} = \frac{24}{2.4869} = 9.651\ or\ \$9,651$$

Project X has a higher EAA than Project Y, which indicates a higher value per year delivered and hence, should be chosen for investment.

9.2 A different way of prioritising: The Draw-down Method

At the beginning of this framework, in section **1.4 Delegation, approvals & thresholds,** we discussed ways of managing project funding through a process where projects continuously come back to the various committees or delegates for further funding. This is known as the *draw-down method.*

In practice, the way that the *draw-down method* works is:

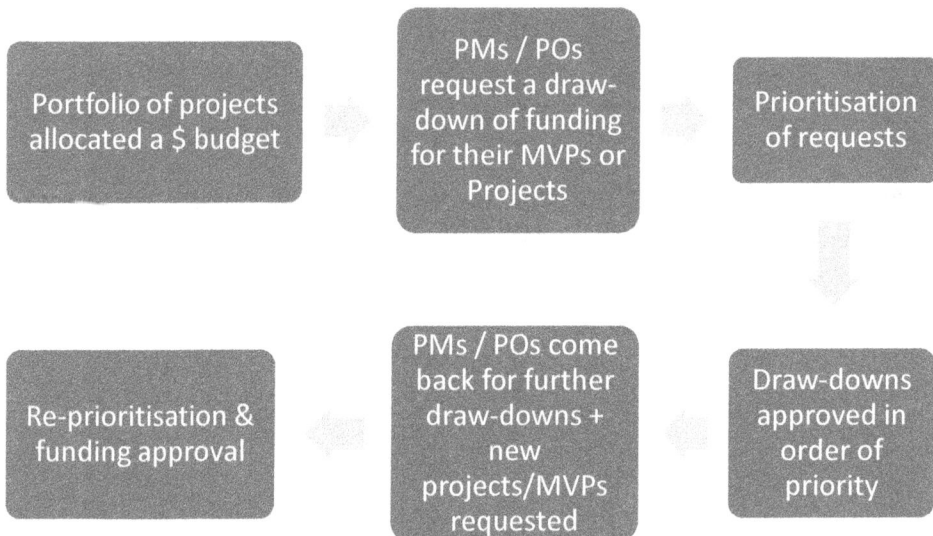

Portfolio of projects allocated a $ budget	PMs / POs request a draw-down of funding for their MVPs or Projects	Prioritisation of requests
Re-prioritisation & funding approval	PMs / POs come back for further draw-downs + new projects/MVPs requested	Draw-downs approved in order of priority

This method can be used for both *Agile and Waterfall Delivery Approaches* to manage portfolio prioritisation.

A number of pit-falls and challenges to note when using this method:
- *Amortisation and depreciation*
  As mentioned in previous sections of this framework, the lack of consideration for P&L impact can have the projects and subsequently the project portfolio run into issues in later years of investment into projects. For example, if only project cash cost draw-down is given consideration, eventually all the various projects that have been capitalised in prior years will be written-down through depreciation and/or amortisation, meaning the P&L allocation required for a

particular year can be vastly different to the cash. This mismatch becomes a problem if left unmanaged.

- *Prioritisation in practice*

  It can be much easier said than done when continuous re-prioritisation of projects is required. The potential challenges here are the ever-changing criteria as to what becomes a priority for an organisation. Some aspects for consideration when continuously re-prioritising projects:

  1. The continuous stop-start or pivoting can mean nothing gets done. Hence, ensuring re-prioritisation is done in long enough intervals for projects or MVPs to deliver value.
  2. Consistent criteria by which priority is determined and not ever changing.
  3. Being able to analyse whether the drawn-down projects are in fact delivering the promised ROI or value.

- *Analysis paralysis*

  Because attributing benefits to projects can be a challenging task, it is tempting to go into 'analysis mode', whereby significant resources are used on conducting an analysis on whether the draw-down already made is bringing in the required value. This framework recommends that clear drivers of value are established for the project or MVP draw-downs. If the drivers are deemed to be achieved, then this would generally indicate that the project or MVP is heading in the right direction. Only the larger investments should have a proper analysis conducted. This follows the lean approach of the 80/20 rule, whereby the Accounting function must allow room for experimentation and failure in its project portfolio.

9.3 Scaled Agile Framework (SAFe)

The Scaled Agile Framework (SAFe) adds another layer of consideration and potential complexity to both projects and organisations. If an organisation uses SAFe to drive value and teams are structured in a way that is recommended by SAFe, then essentially the way that project portfolios are to be funded is driven by value streams and the teams within those value streams.

Weighted Shortest Job First[9]

In a dynamic and lean environment, where projects are often referred to as jobs, activities or tasks (e.g. epics, stories, features), a prioritisation model such as the Weighted Shortest Job First (WSJF) can bring significant value to the organisation. The WSJF is a prioritisation model used to sequence jobs to produce maximum economic benefit.

In SAFe, WSJF is calculated as:

WSFJ = Cost of Delay (CoD) / Job Size

= (User-Business Value + Time Criticality + Risk Reduction and/or Opportunity Enablement) / Job Duration

Agile Release Trains (ARTs) provide an ongoing, continuous flow of work that makes up the Enterprise's incremental development effort. It avoids the overhead and delays caused by the start-stop-start nature of traditional projects, where authorisations and phase gates control the program and its economics.

While this continuous flow model speeds the delivery of value and keeps the system lean, priorities must be updated continuously to provide the best economic outcomes. In a flow-based system, job sequencing, rather than theoretical, individual job/project return on investment, produces the best result. To that end, WSJF is used to prioritise backlogs by calculating the relative CoD and job size (a proxy for the duration). Using WSJF at Program Increment boundaries continuously updates backlog priorities based on user and business value, time factors, risk, opportunity enablement, and effort. WSJF also conveniently and automatically ignores sunk costs, a fundamental principle of Lean economics (Scaled Agile, Inc., 2018).

For the WSJF model to be used, an environment conducive of this way of working is required. As recommended by Leffingwell (2017), there are several steps that an organisation requires to consider in order to implement portfolio management from a financial perspective. We will provide commentary on how these steps fit into the wider part of this framework and the potential challenges these have in practice:

---

[9] Weighted Shortest Job First © 2018, Scaled Agile, Inc. Reproduced with permission.

1. *Fund value streams, not projects:* this is very similar to the draw-down method discussed above, however, rather than directly drawing down for actual projects or MVPs, the value stream draws down on funding to deliver. The challenges to be considered:

   - Benefits (or in this case business and financial value) tracking becomes an even further challenge.
   - This step assumes that the Accounting function is willing or ready for lean-agile accounting within the rest of the business. Experience has shown that for most organisations this kind of change will mean some form of *hybrid accounting* or a move to *lean accounting*, as discussed in **2.1 Business Case vs Lean Canvas,** in order to accommodate this environment.
   - Cost of delay for many organisations may be an issue, however, ensuring the right solution is chosen for the business problem at hand is also an exercise that has its worth i.e. "measure twice, cut once."

2. *Establish portfolio flow*: this step directly relates to the requirement of business cases or lean canvases to manage portfolio flow, as discussed in **Step 2: Planning.**

3. *Forecast predictably:* as discussed in multiple examples in this framework, this can be challenging. If the organisation is working on projects that are largely based on prior experiences, then forecasting predictably is doable. However, *Agile delivery approach* in this book predominantly refers to Scrum, which is a "framework for product development in a complex problem space chosen to deliver largely complex projects" (Bennett, 2017). This means that in forecasting for Scrum projects there may not be prior experiences to rely upon.

4. *Fund innovation like a lean start-up:* the *draw-down method* works in exactly this way. See above.

5. *Budget value streams dynamically:* this step refers to an organisation's budgets requiring adjustment to business case or lean canvas budgets. This framework agrees with this requirement, however, notes the

challenges called out in step *1. Fund value streams, not projects,* where the accounting environment must accommodate this business choice.

6. *Manage Capex & Opex:* as discussed in multiple sections of this framework, due consideration for capitalisation and expenditure is a statutory and regulatory requirement. Noting that Leffingwell's (2017) presentation refers to US GAAP[10] regulatory and statutory requirements, whereas this framework largely refers to IFRS.

Noting, in practice, SAFe is largely used in Technology environments and may not be appropriate for every organisation.

9.4 Earned value & graphical representation

When assessing projects from a portfolio perspective, we look at whether the current portfolio of project investment brings in the expected earned value and strategic benefits. One of the easiest ways to represent this information in a snapshot view is using a graphical representation called "JAWS". JAWS shows the existing difference between income and expenses in the organisation (the wider the gap between the two, the better) and what it will look like if all the projects currently in motion achieve their expected benefits. It considers any benefit erosion that may happen as projects get cancelled or placed on the backlog. Please see *Example 3.3* below.

---

[10] United States' Generally Accepted Accounting Principles (US GAAP), which are largely looked after by the Financial Accounting Standards Board (FASB) dictate various accounting standards in the USA.

Example 3.3:

Company A has the following:

- Average income of $100m and expenses of $50m per annum.
- Its strategy is to increase income to $110m and decrease expenses to $40m per annum within the next 3 years.
- Its annual project portfolio budget is $20m, and it expects to achieve this target.

Please see the graphical representation below:

Company A JAWS

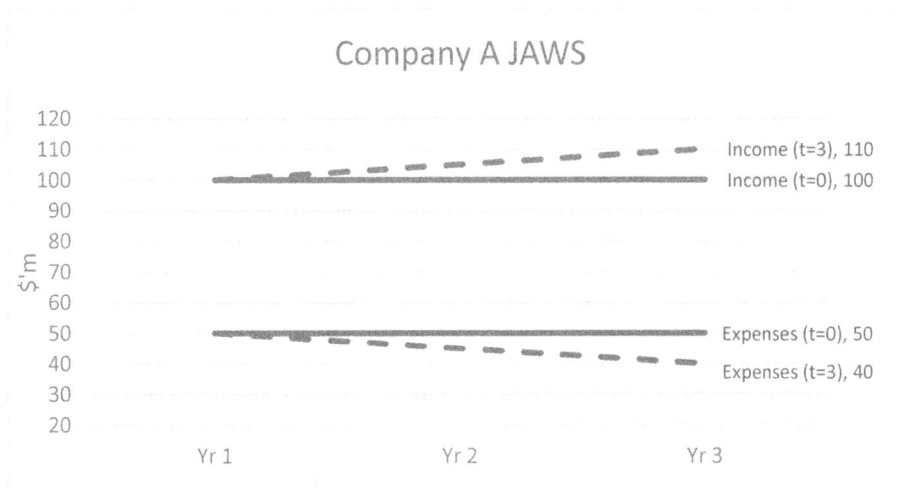

In order to achieve the above, the $20m annual project investment must bring in the corresponding benefits that not only pay for the project but achieve the required targets.

9.5 Resource constraints & overflow

The other issue often faced in portfolio project management is related to resource management and the organisation's ability to ramp up or ramp down on resources when required. The fluid nature of projects means that resources must be flexible enough to step in and out of projects when required. The challenge is to track whether the organisation has resource constraints or resource overflow at any given time. KPIs based on resource utilisation are one way to ensure that resources' time is not wasted, but this is not always helpful if there are not enough projects underway.

How fast or slow the organisation can ramp up or down at any given time for projects can be a strong indicator of the processes in place. Slow and onerous processes can cost organisations significant amounts of money i.e. if the project ROI is not achieved on time, benefits may be eroded, or keeping staff under-utilised will mean additional unexpected cost to BAU. This framework recommends a review of the current processes in place to achieve optimisation; as well as, resource management systems in place to help track utilisation and expected workload.

9.6 Portfolio Considerations

As mentioned in *7.2 Tracking Benefits and OPEX,* portfolios of projects may have significant interdependencies and delivery relationships which may lead to the delivery of interdependent benefits and/or OPEX (which can lead to double counting of benefits/OPEX). To understand these relationships, the Project Management Office (PMO), Project teams and Project Accountants need to work together to track these relationships.

Many organisations keep registers of these interdependencies and relationships in hope that these will be considered when projects are being embarked upon. Unfortunately, these registers are rarely looked at and kept updated as new relationships come up through the duration of the various projects. Instead, this framework recommends that project management forums and systems are used to continually talk about where these interdependencies and relationships exist. Often a live and interactive session involving groups of project managers and product owners can achieve better relationships and understanding of the existing reliance.

Just like for individual projects, the analysis of risks, opportunities and insights for the entire portfolio of projects should be conducted. The reason behind doing this, in addition to individual projects, is these give a holistic picture of what is currently being achieved and provides information around higher level risks and opportunities that may impact the entire portfolio. These may require mitigation from the Executive Board and may drive indications to the organisation's investors whether their funds are being utilised appropriately.

This framework recommends that this type of portfolio analysis is done if the organisation is investing in more than 10 individual independent projects.

KEY TAKEAWAYS

- Deciding on which projects to start, stop and continue needs to be an ongoing exercise that the organisation embarks upon to manage its opportunity cost.

- Equivalent annual annuity (EAA) is a technique that converts a project's NPV into a uniform series of cash flows, enabling the comparison of projects with different project lifecycles and risk profiles, based on the annual value that they add (or based on being repeatable in perpetuity).

- JAWS is a graphical representation that shows the difference between income and expenses in the organisation and what it will look like if all the projects currently in motion achieve their expected benefits.

- Inappropriate resource management can be very costly for an organisation if it cannot quickly ramp up or down depending on project portfolio needs.

- Project interdependencies and relationships must be considered and continuously managed in order to avoid benefits erosion.

- Analysis of risks, opportunities and insights must be done for the entire project portfolio, as well as, significant individual projects.

Step 10: Review and improvement

The one step that is often overlooked in both Waterfall and Agile delivery approaches is the review of key learnings or retrospectives from delivery and financial processes. The main reason these reviews are left undone is often related to lack of time. This framework, along with a multitude of other literature, urges project teams to conduct this activity. If left undone, mistakes and failures will undoubtedly repeat themselves.

The above paragraph refers to project review and implementation of financial processes as part of the post-implementation review (PIR), for waterfall delivery approach, and retrospectives, as part of agile delivery approach.

- *PIR* is a documented assessment and review of what has been delivered by the project and any recommended improvements in future processes. PIRs are undertaken after the project is completed or during the time of handover to BAU. The purpose of a PIR is to document key learnings to assist future projects decision-making and provide process improvement suggestions. Below are key review areas of a PIR:
  1. Ascertain if the project scope was delivered
  2. Planned levels of benefits delivered
  3. Length of time, efficiency approach and costs reviewed
  4. Engagement with third-parties finalised
  5. Executive Board, Project Board and Sponsor engagements finalised
  6. Solutions for issues managed and mitigated
  7. Management of contingency finalised
  8. Lessons learnt documented or discussed

The PIR is generally undertaken by an external member to the project team, who is independent of the project. This ensures avoidance of conflict of interest, transparency, management of opportunity cost and consistent decision making.

- *Retrospectives* are to be done at the end of each Sprint. They are the most important and least appreciated practices, however, are crucial contributors to the continuous improvement that Scrum offers. Within a retrospective, teams examine what is happening, analyse the way they work, identify ways to improve, and make plans to implement those improvements into future Sprints and existing processes (Cohn & Jeffries, 2013).

During these reviews, the Project team's relationship with the Accounting division must also be reviewed, as project accounting methodology must also evolve and continuously learn to adapt to the projects' world.

Continuous process improvement within projects and accounting processes is a must, to achieve simplification, optimisation and strength in relationships among all project stakeholders involved.

KEY TAKEAWAYS

- Process implementation review is a documented assessment and review of what has been delivered by the project.

- Retrospectives are to be done at the end of each Sprint and Epic.

- Continuous process improvement within projects and accounting processes is a must, to achieve simplification, optimisation and strength in relationships among all project stakeholders involved.

Conclusion

Forgetting the Money: 10 step framework to harness true project value has been developed with over a decade of experience with substantial industry input from the project accounting community. This book summarises this knowledge into 10 steps to provide recommendations for the wider project community including organisations, project teams and accountants involved in projects.

This Framework has concentrated on financial success of projects regardless of the project delivery approach chosen. By implementing the 10 steps of this framework, you are stepping toward more transparent decision-making, reduction in financial risk and increase in likelihood of project success.

At the time of writing this in 2018, there is no standardisation in the project industry of how to account for and help projects from a financial stand-point to decrease the amount of project failure in the industry.

The time has come for project professionals to embrace their financial project value and not merely maintain projects. Knowing your project's true value is your best friend to know exactly what is going on and what needs to be done. Using this financial information you can improve your decision making and project impact and prove your projects' true value.

I believe that this book provides a useful overview of the necessary requirements for project financial success, as you get to implement some of these steps.

Please get in touch directly through Project Accounting Australia (www.projectaccounting.com.au) for feedback, suggestions and comments.

Glossary

Agile (delivery) approach: is an incremental approach to the delivery of a project. The project team start off with a simplistic project design and then begin to work on small modules. Each module will include elements of design, development and testing in order to deliver a stand-alone feature.

Amortisation: Spreading the costs of an <u>intangible</u> asset across multiple years over its useful life.

Capitalisation: is the term used to refer to the recognition or creation of an asset. As an example – by constructing a building, we are creating an asset, therefore; the costs associated with building this asset are capitalisable. This is a widely used term around the world and is predominantly used by Accountants to describe various circumstances surrounding asset creation and/or recognition. To **capitalise** is to create an asset.

Carded Rates: These rates are often called *charge out rates* – the rate at which a labour resource charges their time to the Project. The main reasons behind these rates are confidentiality of salary disclosures and ease of forecasting/budgeting project cost with relatively simple calculations.

Data visualisation: is a field that studies the human response to information and the best way to present data in a visual and meaningful manner for ease of decision-making.

Delivery Team: according to Waterfall handles the delivery of the project's product within the scope, time, quality and cost. According to Agile, is responsible to deliver the committed delivery in time and with the defined quality. It is a stand-alone body self-managing the delivery.

Depreciation: Spreading the costs of a <u>tangible</u> asset across multiple years over its useful life.

Estimate at Completion (EAC): the forecast cost of the project inclusive of actuals to date i.e. Actual cost spent + Forecast spend = EAC.

Executive Board: this is the key leadership, who allocate the funding for investment into projects. This team maintains accountability to the shareholders of the organisation and handles disclosure of investments made. This team will appoint a Project Board or a Project Sponsor to take responsibility for individual projects or programs.

Expensing (Writing off): a project cost is to recognise that the cost is incurred in the current financial period rather than deferring out to a future date via the creation of an asset on the Balance Sheet.

Financial Accounting: gathers and summarizes financial data to prepare financial reports such as balance sheet and income statement for the organisation's management, investors, lenders, suppliers, tax authorities, and other stakeholders.

First-year OPEX: is the additional cost that an organisation incurs in the first-year of the project's lifecycle due to the project's deliverable. It is derived due to an action that a project has implemented.

Hybrid accounting environment: can work in a variety of ways. It is a general combination of both Standards and Lean accounting ways of working, which will co-exist in some form of process for the finance function.

Hybrid (delivery) approach: is a mix of both Agile and Waterfall delivery approaches. The optimum project combination incorporates significant planning and quality assessment input early in the development process. This is done in order to mitigate errors while introducing Agile processes to the release schedule and user feedback opportunities, allowing for faster and more controlled improvements.

Impairment Testing: is thinking about whether the asset is still used and to what extent after project completion. Reduction in derived or expected benefits may also indicate asset impairment. There are very strict guidelines around *impairment testing* of assets set by various Accounting Standards Boards and advice should be sought around your locally applicable rules.

Lean accounting environment: lean accounting is KPI based accounting that seeks to eliminate waste from a company's capital resources by applying lean principles to the company's financial functions.

Management Accounting: the process of preparing management reports and accounts that provide accurate and timely financial and statistical information required by managers to make day-to-day and short-term decisions.

Materiality: significance, particularly with relation to a transaction. *Materiality* for projects is different for every organisation and is often driven by the Executive Board and/or the Accounting Division.

Month-end: refers to the accounting monthly cycle, where the accounting general ledger is finalised for the month and accounting reports are released.

Permanent variance: a lasting saving or overspend to the project.

Product Owner*:* handles the interface between the Delivery Team and the stakeholders of the project i.e. Project Sponsor. The key responsibility of this role is for the return on investment (ROI) of the project.

Project: a separate temporary individualised entity set up for the purpose of delivering one or more business products.

Project accounting: an accounting field that requires the knowledge of management accounting, financial accounting, cross-functional involvement, and understanding of project delivery approaches used by the business.

Project Board: handles the overall direction and management of the project within the constraints set out by the Executive Board. This team is accountable for the success of the project.

Project Manager: handles the day-to-day management of the project within the constraints set out by the Project Board.

Project Sponsor: is the business entity, whether a division or an individual interested in the successful delivery of the project for the business. This role mainly exists in larger organisations creating a buffer between the Executive Board and the Product Owner.

Run rate: the quantitative amount that is achieved through a consistent realisation of the same result every month.

Scrum Master: ensures that the Delivery Team adheres to the Scrum theory, practices and rules.

Skills-based subdivision: some organisational structures split teams by skill sets; these can be Value Streams or Platforms. This is argued to be conducive of enabling a more agile working environment. Splitting teams by skill sets can be quite a complex exercise, especially in existing organisations for whom the concept is new. However, the key here is to ensure clear team structures are set without overcomplicated matrix structures enabling a clearer cross-functional agile working environment.

Standard accounting environment: this is referring to the historical ways of working when accounting for business activity, i.e. strong reliance on guidance from standards-based reporting without consideration for project delivery approaches.

Timing variance: a temporary saving or overspend to the project.

Waterfall (delivery) approach: is a sequential design process for delivery of a project. This means that as each stage is completed, the project team moves on to the next one. As this process is sequential, once a stage has been completed, the project team can't go back to a previous stage.

Weighted Shortest Job First (WSJF): The WSJF is a prioritisation model used to sequence jobs to produce maximum economic benefit.

Writing off (expensing): a project cost is to recognise that the cost is incurred in the current financial period rather than deferring out to a future date via the creation of an asset on the Balance Sheet.

References

Agile Alliance, 2015. *Relative Estimation.* [Online]
Available at: https://www.agilealliance.org/glossary/relative-estimation/
[Accessed 24 February 2017].

Agile42, 2016. *Scrum Roles.* [Online]
Available at: http://www.agile42.com/en/agile-info-center/scrum-roles/
[Accessed 12 September 2016].

AXELOS Limited, 2014. *Managing Successful Projects within PRINCE2®.* 4 ed.
Norwich: TSO.

Bennett, S., 2017. *Strategy, Politics, Competition & Knowledge - Lessons in Advanced Product Backlog Management.* Melbourne: Scrum Australia.

Bloch, M., Blumberg, S. & Laartz, J., 2012. *Delivering large-scale IT projects on time, on budget, and on value.* [Online]
Available at: http://www.mckinsey.com/business-functions/digital-mckinsey/our-insights/delivering-large-scale-it-projects-on-time-on-budget-and-on-value
[Accessed 19 February 2017].

Boyte-White, C., 2016. *What is the formula for calculating net present value (NPV) in Excel?.* [Online]
Available at: http://www.investopedia.com/ask/answers/021115/what-formula-calculating-net-present-value-npv-excel.asp
[Accessed 7 November 2016].

Brown, D. et al., 2016. CPA Program. In: *Strategic Management Accounting.* Geelong: Deakin University, pp. 489-565.

Business Dictionary, n.d. *Business Dictionary.* [Online]
Available at: http://www.businessdictionary.com
[Accessed 25 June 2018].

Cohn, M., 2014. *How Many Hours Is a Story Point Worth?.* [Online]
Available at: https://www.scrumalliance.org/community/spotlight/mike-

cohn/june-2014/how-many-hours-is-a-story-point-worth
[Accessed 14 September 2017].

Cohn, M. & Jeffries, R., 2013. *Essential Scrum.* 3rd ed. Ann Arbor, Michigan: Addison-Wesley.

Finch, C., 2007. Why Project Accounting?. *Strategic Finance, Institute of Management Accountants,* Volume November 2007, pp. 25-29.

Goldstein, I., 2014. *Scrum Shortcuts without Cutting Corners.* Crawfordsville: Addison-Wesley.

Investopedia, 2017. *Scenario / What-If Analysis.* [Online]
Available at: http://www.investopedia.com/walkthrough/corporate-finance/4/project-analysis/scenario.aspx
[Accessed 29 May 2017].

Investopedia, n.d. *Internal Rate of Return - IRR.* [Online]
Available at: http://www.investopedia.com/terms/i/irr.asp
[Accessed 4 March 2017].

Kahneman, D., 2011. *Thinking Fast and Slow.* New York: Farrar, Strauss and Giroux.

Lachal, J., McNeill, C., Tong, L. & McCoy, K., 2016. Project Accounting. *Business Insights,* September, Issue 39, pp. 1-3.

Leffingwell, D., 2017. *Financial Aspects of Lean Portfolio Management,* San Antonio: SAFe Summit 2017.

Maurya, A., 2012. *Why Lean Canvas vs Business Model Canvas?.* [Online]
Available at: https://leanstack.com/why-lean-canvas/
[Accessed 24 Oct 2016].

Parmenter, D., 2016. *Lean planning & forecasting for the 21st Century.* Sydney, Chartered Accountants Australia & NZ (CAANZ).

Ries, E., 2011. *The Lean Startup.* USA: Crown Publishing Group.

Scaled Agile, Inc., 2018. *Weighted Shortest Job First.* [Online]
Available at: https://www.scaledagileframework.com/wsjf/
[Accessed 7 May 2018].

Sweeney, M., 2014. *Agile vs Waterfall: Which Method is more Successful?,* s.l.: Clearcode.

The Access Group, 2016. *Capterra Project Management Blog.* [Online]
Available at: https://blog.capterra.com/surprising-project-management-statistics/
[Accessed 15 December 2017].

Warner, M., 2017. *The Project Management Blueprint.* [Online]
Available at: http://www.theprojectmanagementblueprint.com/?p=244
[Accessed 17 May 2017].

WhatIs.com, 2012. *WhatIs.com.* [Online]
Available at: http://whatis.techtarget.com/definition/business-case
[Accessed 24 Oct 2016].

Williams, T., 2014. *Stop Start Continue: Thinking Provocatively About The Past, Present & Future Of Employee Engagement.* Auckland: seriouspeople.

Index

www.ingramcontent.com/pod-product-compliance
Lightning Source LLC
Chambersburg PA
CBHW051219200326
41519CB00025B/7172